POPULATION
A PROBLEM FOR DEMOCRACY

POPULATION

A Problem for Democracy

THE GODKIN LECTURES, 1938

By

GUNNAR MYRDAL

GLOUCESTER, MASS.

PETER SMITH

1962

REPRINTED, 1962
BY PERMISSION OF
HARVARD UNIVERSITY PRESS

EDWIN LAWRENCE GODKIN

1831–1902

Edwin Lawrence Godkin, editor of *The Nation* and the New York *Evening Post*, was born in Ireland of English stock, and took his degree at Queen's College, Belfast, in 1851. He published a *History of Hungary* and was associated with the London *Daily News* and the Belfast *Northern Whig* before coming to America in 1856. Here his letters to the *Daily News* on American public affairs attracted attention and prepared him for the task he assumed in 1865 as first editor of *The Nation*, to which he gave a scholarly quality, a breadth of view, and a moral tone that brought it recognition as one of the best weeklies in the English-speaking world. In 1881 *The Nation* became the weekly edition of the New York *Evening Post*, of which Godkin was made editor in chief in 1883. From that time until his retirement in 1900 he exercised an influence on public opinion out of all proportion to the circulation of his paper. Editors throughout the country, whether in sympathy with his views or not, watched for his editorials on all important issues. He was exceptionally well read in economics, history, and political theory, believed wholeheartedly in democracy, owed allegiance to no person or party, and was vigorous and fearless in expression. In 1903, by a gift to Harvard University, his friends established "The Godkin Lectures on the Essentials of Free Government and the Duties of the Citizen" in appreciation of his long and disinterested service to the country of his adoption and in the hope of stimulating that spirit of independent thought and devotion to the public service which characterized his career.

PREFACE

America has the unique strategic advantage — if it could only be capitalized — that several of its social and political problems are maturing to acuteness a couple of decades later than in some of the older democracies of northern and western Europe, among them my own country, Sweden. Certainly this is true of the problems dealt with in this book. America has still an aggregate fertility which nearly matches its mortality, even when corrected for the factor of age structure — although it is now steadily declining and although during the decline there have developed within the nation reproduction differences between regions, racial groups, and classes of perhaps a still more alarming nature. And in America social policy is only in *statu nascendi*.

This being the situation, the professional social engineer is naturally tempted to indulge in wishful visions of how America might profit from the experiences of Europe. At least, it should not be necessary for America to remake all our mistakes. In the older countries referred to, social policy has been growing as some of the old cathedrals grew: chapels and towers were added in different periods and in different styles, walls were moved, windows opened, and the general plan, if there ever was one, was lost for long periods. We are now constantly searching for means of rationalizing and coördinating the historical outgrowth into some sort of integrated system. The naïve vision of the social engineer is that here in the New World a modern, rational, functionalistic structure of policy could be planned from the start, based on the final conclusions but not repeating all of the earlier experimentations in darkness.

In the large this vision will probably turn out to be an illusion. Nations, like individuals, insist on their opportunity to experience their own trials and errors. We seem never to learn much from history, at least not from other people's histories. On closer view this is also rather natural. Social policy has to be adapted to the circumstantial setting of each country and each period, and, still more important, it has to be based on political ideals and articulated interests which can develop only in organic relation to the growth of this policy itself.

Nevertheless, if it were possible to forecast broadly the secular trend of such a basic factor as population development, and if it were possible also to wring certain generalizations from other nations' experiences about how such a trend remolds the problematics of social policy, this should give the ideologist and the social engineer in America a perspective in the one important direction — toward the future — and thereby also assure a firmer basis for more rational planning.

In the field of population policy, to be more specific, it ought not to be necessary that in America as, e.g., in Sweden and England, organized efforts to spread rational birth control should pursue a largely negative propaganda until the very moment when the population development itself comes to demand the integration in it of more positive ideals. If an early redirection of Neo-Malthusian strivings could be accomplished, this would break down the barriers against rational birth control and make it easier to win for it its natural place in public health activity. In America it should be possible to make public opinion aware so early of the desirability of keeping up aggregate fertility that reproduction will not, as with us, have first to dive down very deeply before measures can be planned to reverse the trend. In America efforts to level out the great and obnoxious fertility differences between the over-fertile poor strata and the under-fertile middle and upper strata could be instigated before that final diving, and, consequently, the leveling process could be directed upon a higher plane than with us.

As to social policy generally, it should be possible in America to build up the mainly symptomatic and curative policy which belongs to its first stage — relief and social security — on a plan that would afford a basis, rather than a hindrance, for its later completion into a prophylactic and preventive family policy. Among other things this would presuppose that in the present early stage of the very founding of a social policy in this country a thorough discussion — such as we have not had in Europe — of the paramount problem of principles would be carried on: e.g., whether, and to what extent, this policy ought to work with means tests and other economic limitations, or be based on the principle of civic cooperation and pooling of individual funds; and whether, and to what extent, it ought to be planned to give allowance in cash or in kind. The last-mentioned problem is one of relative efficiency and cost, and concerns, furthermore, the integration of social policy in a wider economic policy. It is also a problem of how to utilize limited public funds. If too large portions of the public budgets and the citizens' compulsory contributions are mortgaged in social security schemes and for other cash doles, it might be difficult to release funds for the prophylactic family policy in kind — to raise directly standards of housing, nutrition, health, and education — which will be called forth by the political consequences of the population trend, if not earlier.

This much to explain why the author, when invited to give four lectures at Harvard University in the Spring of 1938 under the Godkin Foundation and under its general rubric, The Essentials of Free Government and the Duties of the Citizen, ventured to propose as the topic for the lectures: The Population Problem and Social Policy. I am fully aware of the probability that the problems dealt with in this little volume, which comprises in slightly rearranged form the content of these lectures, are not going to be acute in this country in the near future, except in the minds of a very small minority of people with a long-range interest in political questions. I have viewed the problems very much as they have appeared on the Swedish horizon, where for various reasons they have reached an early actuality, but have kept the general perspective of western democratic industrial society in mind. In the present publication I have retained the lecture form and also the intentionally general and nontechnical approach. I have had to be content with the presentation of some broad principles and with stopping short of the real problems of social engineering.

These principles have been developed, worked out in their details and as to their socio-technical consequences, and partly also tested out in political appeal and action in a collaboration between my wife, Alva Myrdal, and myself (*Kris i befolkningsfrågan*, Stockholm, 1934). She is now preparing a much more complete analysis of the whole complex of problems involved. In this forthcoming book a comprehensive and detailed treatment of the specific measures of social family policy is intended, while my lectures do not go further than the statement of some of the general principles for such a policy. I have hesitated much over the question as to whether under these circumstances my lectures are worth publishing. When they now, under the kind urging of the Harvard University Press, are nevertheless published, it is in the hope that they will serve as an introduction to the subject, particularly as to the mechanics of political attitudes in the population problem and as to the economic effects of the population trend.

G. M.

NEW YORK
August, 1939

CONTENTS

POPULATION
A PROBLEM FOR DEMOCRACY

I

BACKGROUND

DISCUSSIONS of the population problem have always had the capacity to stir up public sentiment much more than most other problems.

For one thing this problem happens to touch spheres of individual morals which in western civilization have traditionally been the focus of interest for preachers and moralists: the relation between the sexes, mating and marriage, propagation and the family. In our cultural heritage "morals" means specifically and particularly "sexual morals" — and so according not only to Puritan tradition but to Christian tradition broadly. The ordinary citizen in our type of culture is complex-ridden in his sexual life, and this emotional charge is carried over to the scientific discussion of the contiguous social problem, both because the scientist, as a person, is mostly, in this and other respects, quite ordinary himself; and because in any case he has to take great care about how the huge mass of ordinarians represented in civic organizations, pressure groups, political parties and legislatures, since they are his neighbors and generally constitute his social milieu, react to what he says. Thus the population problem has acquired the rank — and the peculiar constraints — of a matter of conscience. And this far down in personal morality social problems usually do not reach.

It must, however, instantly be emphasized that this contact with the sphere of individual sexual ethics has, for the most part, only given an emotional load to the discussion of the population problem and induced the peculiar intellectual constraints which we presently will comment upon. It has scarcely contributed much to the political content of the issues involved. That is, at least, if, as in this preliminary survey, we keep to the higher level of this discussion, where opinions are thoroughly considered and rationally integrated into systematic social thought, the political contents of opinions in the population problem are not to be inferred from this contact. The combats over the population issue are ultimately concerned with the broad questions of social welfare and economic equality. These combats are therefore to be properly understood only as part of the broad front in the incessant struggle since the eighteenth century between reactionary and radical social goals and class interests.

In fact, the discussion of the population problem seems at all times and in all places to be more strongly dominated by these volitional elements of political ideals and interests than any other part of the established body of social and economic thinking. Here, as in perhaps no other branch of social theorizing, the wish is very often father to the thought. Population theory has necessarily always been less "pure" than other theories. More potently than in any other field have the different authors been swayed by their political ideals — even, and above all, when they have not been conscious themselves that they were merely expounding their political faiths, and even when what they have said has contained nothing which explicitly informs their readers of the underlying political basis of their theories.

The political element in population theory,

moreover, has not only been the basic, if sometimes hidden, essence of this special theory as it has appeared at different times and in different social settings, but it also, in a quite powerful fashion, has determined the political tendencies inherent in other economic doctrines outside the population field. At crucial points in the development of economic theory, the population question has been the axis around which the ideological basis has turned. I know of nothing more dramatic in the evolution of social doctrine through time than the great secular swings of scientific opinion in the population problem and the synchronous, and we might say, as I will show, the consequent, changing currents in general social speculation.

These statements are not to be understood as implying that thinking about the population issue has been nothing more than a direct reflection of political wishes and an obedient vehicle enabling these volitional tendencies to sway the entire system of social doctrines in their direction. The matter is not so simple. To a large extent this thinking has at the same time always been rational and founded upon factual premises. As will be pointed out, the actual fertility rates at the close of the eighteenth century and the then dominant political valuations and prevalent social conditions, specifically as to level of living in the broad lower income strata, should rationally have led to the Malthusian theory, particularly, furthermore, since birth control was *a priori* considered a sin and, anyhow, not a very practicable proposal. These premises were, however, equally factual a generation earlier, and it thus needs to be explained why the theory had not already been clearly expounded. The explanation should be looked for in the radical optimistic slant of political thinking in the epoch of enlightenment as well as in the more incomplete and unsystematized knowledge of relevant facts. On the other hand, it is equally clear that the present trend of fertility must lead to radical political proposals implying fundamental changes in the economic basis for the institution of the family, provided the political premise is accepted that depopulation should be checked. This is the rational element in the political discussion of population to be expected during the next few decades. The volitional element is visible in the fact that students with a positive inclination toward public interference will be apt to point out these political conclusions, while students with opposite inclinations will try to evade them or even feel inclined to abstain from thinking over the whole issue.

From what has already been said it appears that a close study of the history of population theory in its relation to political thinking should be paramount. In these lectures not more than the broadest outlines can be attempted.[1]

The cameralists and mercantilists on the whole looked upon population, as they did upon the whole social problem, from the narrow political point of view of what was in the best interest of the State or the Crown. The social welfare concept was not yet born. With the autocratic concept as its basic primary desideratum, it appeared to them as naturally desirable that labor should be abundant and cheap. They favored a large population. Their population theory, like their other theories,

[1] See Myrdal, *Das politische Element in die nationalökonomische Doktrinbildung* (Berlin, 1932).

had its major premise — and from this its theoretical validity — in its character of being a social plan bent upon producing the most advantageous conditions for the commercial exploitation of a land and a people in the interest of the Prince. Looked on as a theory of social engineering, their population doctrine can hardly be said to have been "wrong" if it is judged as proceeding from their political premise and the factual conditions of their time.

During the eighteenth century, the philosophy of natural rights and utilitarianism dethroned the prince or the state and replaced it with the people as the ultimate value in social and economic speculation. This was an enormous change in the whole foundation of all social philosophy. Hereafter all economic doctrines, before anything else, had to be based upon a consideration of what would be for the good of all. That remains today our great inheritance from the eighteenth century.

The very foundation of political economy thereafter, as until lately, contained a strong radical flavor. All men, said the natural rights philosophers, were born equal. They all had the same rights. This principle was inscribed in those famous declarations which were regarded as laying the foundation for a new society in the United States and in France: the Declaration of Independence, in 1776, and la Déclaration des Droits de l'Homme, in 1789. From the natural rights philosophy was inherited also the labor theory of value, the strong radical import of which Karl Marx was not the first to demonstrate. Only labor was productive and could be a true sanction of property rights. The realization of these natural rights would of necessity have meant an equalization of wealth in society, for, even if capacity to work varies individually, these personal differences are much smaller than, and do not correspond to, existing inequalities in the distribution of wealth.

In utilitarianism, which more and more became the basis of Anglo-Saxon social philosophy, the principle of equality was preserved as an axiomatic postulate: the whole calculus of social welfare was entirely false if each individual was not counted as one, and no one as more than one. With the aid of the theory of decreasing utility, which in a more definite form had already been developed by Bentham and which was taken over by the whole classical school of economists and is even today found in textbooks, one could prove in an "objective" way that the good of all society is increased through equalizing income and wealth among the people and, therefore, through taking from the rich and giving to the poor. Consequently, the classical theory of economics contained in its first principles strongly radical ideas about property rights.

This whole system of thought was in fact built upon the radical ideas which had come to flower in the French Revolution. In the beginning the Revolution was greeted as a victory of reason by all enlightened and many unenlightened spirits throughout the whole world, especially in England, which was the land of lands that nurtured the economic ideology of classical economic liberalism. But when the Revolution took an entirely different direction than had been expected and desired, most good people became terrified. It then became necessary to find some argument through which a more conservative interpretation could be developed. Such an argument certainly could not be discovered in the basic philosophy; on the contrary, it was and remained obstinately radical. In those circles where economic and political thinking was further developed one was not ready to abandon this philosophy completely.

It was thus a matter of hitting upon an argument to rationalize a new swing of ideas in a conservative direction, an argument which would protect the liberal economist's ideological system against its own radical basic principles, which principles could not be abandoned. In this dilemma of acute ideological need Malthus developed his population theory, the most formidable argument for economic conservatism which economic science ever had, or ever has since, procured. Poverty and misery, the theory declared, cannot be blamed upon the ruling system of property rights or other parts of social institutions; they are prescribed by Nature. It may be remarked parenthetically that this is the most profound difference between conservatism and radicalism. Everything depends upon how much one wants to blame heredity and environment respectively. The radical believes that "opportunity makes the thief," but the conservative holds the opposite, that it is the thief who makes the opportunity. The radical says that an open door may tempt a saint; the conservative is inclined to stress the view that the non-saint might be suspected of opening the door. The pessimistic view of human nature is, and has always been, the deepest sense of a conservative argument when it is not openly motivated by the interests of the upper classes, a motivation which, in democracies, has gone more and more out of fashion. The Malthusian theory is no exception.

Malthus thus shifted the blame for misery from Society to Nature, from environment to heredity. The blame heaped upon society by radical thinking during the eighteenth century became, in the hands of Malthus, only a scientific explanation of a necessary evil. Vice and misery, said Malthus, even have a function to fulfill in Nature's great dispensation: to maintain the balance between means of existence and the pressure of population.

The political conclusion is clear in principle: in the long-range view, all social reforms seeking to better the plight of the lower classes are futile. In fact, the Malthusian population theory — as was not usually observed — could be used not only as an argument against reforming the system of distribution for the advantage of the poor, but even as an argument for increasing social protectionism for the advantage of the rich. That is, the masses were always and necessarily doomed to be limited through misery and vice to the available means of existence. The sum of misery and vice was not really increased, according to this long-range view, by limiting the means of existence for the poorer classes. When, nevertheless, the well-being of the comparatively few persons in the intramarginal groups, who were living in prosperity, should be increased through any such perverted social policy, there was, of course, an absolute profit in the social calculus of pleasure and pain to be gained by such measures without any accompanying loss. This most hardened inference, however, was not drawn: one felt satisfied with the system of *laissez faire*.

Classical Manchester liberalism with its strong conservative tendency is thus based upon the Malthus population doctrine. Theoretically, its rejection of radical property reforms cannot be explained and brought to harmonize with the postulates of social philosophy, which are the basis also of the Manchester system, without the help of this doctrine. Malthus' theory is naturally only to be understood as a manifestation of the broad swing away from political radicalism, in the opposite direction of political reaction, which later, after the Napoleonic Wars, flourished in all fields of culture. This reactionary change, which in politics was represented by the Holy Alliance and the Restoration, in jurisprudence by the school of the historical jurists, in literature and philosophy by Romanticism, and in all the other fields by similar phenomena, constitutes one of the most interesting and still far from completely clarified problems in the intellectual history of western civilization. In political economy it was represented by the current of conservative Malthusianism, and the Malthusianism in its turn entwined itself with the whole development of political economy, twisting it for a time in a pessimistic, conservative direction. I am not overlooking the reservations and qualifications which Malthus introduced in later editions of his essay and which were also elaborated by Ricardo and his pupils. But in spite of these vestiges of hesitation and afterthought, the population theory remained pessimistic and was instrumental for conservative political conclusions during the whole epoch of classical economy.

Malthus was certainly "right" if his postulate about the rate of procreation and the consequent population pressure was accepted as a true description of reality and a necessary element of our social system. Therefore, when within a few decades political ideas again took a more radical direction, the Malthusian postulate simply had to be pushed aside. A certain technical development and a redefinition of Malthus' notion of "vices" were the instrument by means of which one was able to escape the conclusion that the masses are doomed to be in an eternal dilemma between vice and misery. Contraception was the argument — and in fact the only possible argument — capable of breaking down the conservative conclusions concerning property rights which Malthus and the whole group of classical economists had drawn, but from which it was now desired to escape. The social liberalism of John Stuart Mill and later the whole neoclassic school required birth control as a necessary part of their system — a system which otherwise would break on the rock of the population problem just as Godwin's and Condorcet's Utopianism had broken down.

When Mill wrote, the decline in the birth rate had not yet set in generally, but the possibilities for "rational birth control" were already sufficient for the purpose of the theory. Here we have, by the way, one of the nicest examples of the way in which theoretical reasoning anticipates technical and social development. Neo-Malthusianism was thereafter implied, and is still implied, in the liberal reformist outlook on economic life. The whole new morality in the field of sexual conduct, which gradually grew up with the practice of Neo-Malthusianism, was functionalistic and experimental. Behavior became realistic and purposeful; in a word, was pragmatic. Corresponding changes in other spheres of personality ran side by side with the changed social environment and cultural milieu which industrialization gradually shaped. Little by little old folkways and mores were broken down; a more secularized personality type developed. It is true that the old bourgeois conventions have endured, though to a great extent only as outer forms. The realities they contain have been changed, and, in the large, these conventions have come to have less secure psychological moorings.

Now that the slow but steady development of birth control has become a truly serious peril for the reproduction of a people, however, the population problem which with Malthus had been a deadly weapon in the service of economic conservatism, and with Mill a constantly menacing obstacle to be overcome in the mild liberal reformism of his inclinations, comes once more to have a fundamentally changed political function. It now becomes what a Swedish economist of the older school has reproachfully but, indeed, very properly called a "crowbar for social reforms" — reforms of a much bolder scope and a fundamentally changed direction than the ones which were dreamt of in Mill's time and which since then, during the liberalist epoch in democratic countries, have been slowly enacted. It is within the frame of this new ideological crisis in the population problem — of which we today are hearing only the first distant rumblings — that the analysis undertaken in these lectures of the political element in the population problem is carried out.

Each population doctrine has in the main been correct if only we grant the major premises of those advocating it: the mercantilists, who wanted the largest possible amount of human material for producing riches; Malthus, who believed that the most cruel sort of self-limitation of the population was inevitable; Mill, who accepted the doctrine that limitation was the problem, but believed that it could be accomplished through the infinitely more humane method of birth control; and we today, who are concerned lest birth control, operating in the social environment created by industrialization and the capitalistic system of distribution, be carried too far. As the mercantilists were right at the time and in view of their own assumptions, as Malthus and Mill were right, so also are we of the present right.

The great material phenomenon behind this

alteration of the political "meaning" of the population problem lies, of course, in the changing rate of human procreation. At present the practical problem in western countries is not, as it was a hundred years ago, the inevitable pressure of population against the limits of the available means of subsistence, nor, as it was fifty years ago, how to substitute birth control for vice and misery as checks on population growth. Today the problem is how to get a people to abstain from not reproducing itself.

I think it is useful, if one is fully to grasp the wide implications which the population problem will have in the near future, to be reminded of these great secular swings of political ideology. I have concerned myself only with that part of this discussion which is carried on by thinkers and scholars. Even on that intellectual level, as I said when I started out, the latitude of differing opinions, and particularly the bitterness of controversy, is tremendously accentuated — on the one hand, because of the exceptionally close association of the population problem with focal points of individual ethical and religious valuations and, on the other hand, because of the ramifying consequences a position taken in this problem has for the burning political questions of how power over and share in the social product shall be imputed to the various social classes, families, and individual citizens in a society. And this intellectual discussion which I am reviewing is in the final analysis hardly more than a leading melody emerging out of the discord of complex-ridden emotions, confusedly sensed class interests, and inarticulate personal cravings of all those millions and millions of non-intellectual human beings in various social circumstances who compose public opinion.

And, as I have said, public opinion is touchy on this very spot. It is, indeed, easy to understand why the scientist, particularly in this problem, and particularly in the present phase of social and political development, seeks an escape in facts. And it is also understandable why he sometimes goes further and distorts the statements of his fact-finding in order to make them less significant to the general public. Thus, to point out one striking example, statisticians and economists seem to have convinced the intelligent layman and, what ought to be more difficult, even themselves, that the present tendency is toward a "mature," "constant," or "stable" population, which is an absolutely unfounded inference from the known facts, if not a flagrant misrepresentation. A milder judgment would perhaps regard such statements as the outgrowth of an overzealous watchfulness in making generalizations. But the point is that these euphemisms have a definite tendency; they wrench truth precisely in one direction — the one which does not bring to the forefront the necessity of drawing a whole complex of practical conclusions in the dangerous fields of public politics and private ethics.

In the present epoch the development of population has such a fatal direction and is fraught with such momentous political consequences, and the popular mind is so nervous for other reasons, that the scientist must be tempted more than ever to indulge in an increasingly minute description without venturing the relevant theoretical analysis and the implied practical (i.e., moral and political) conclusions. The secular change in the amount and character of popular response must also be noted. In Malthus' time the group of persons who took notice of a general discussion of social problems constituted only a very small portion of the people. When J. S. Mill wrote, the proportion had grown, though not considerably; it included the Victorian middle class. (Mill, by the way, was evasive outside the realm of general principles; he never publicly committed himself much on the question of contraception, although a quite unambiguous opinion can be inferred from his announcements of those principles.) In our time the broad masses, from the non-intellectual middle class on down, are increasingly being drawn into participation. They are made acquainted with the highlights of intellectual discussion through adult education, press, and radio; religious and political organizations are articulating their attitudes, sometimes actually manufacturing them, and in any case mobilizing them for pressure purposes.

Remember also that the political conclusions of the present population trend are far more dynamic than hitherto; they mean political interferences on a huge scale. Malthus was, after all, only pleading noninterference and, particularly, the utter hopelessness of social reform, which was not in itself an undesirable doctrine, but quite the contrary, from the point of view of the small upper-class circle which was the sounding board for social theories in his time — although to some it seemed too blunt and cynical a theory. Mill believed in contraception, but the spread of rational birth control could be left to natural forces and particularly to individual initiative, a concept dear to the liberalist middle class. The conclusions from population tendencies of the present call, on the contrary, for political interference of a radical scope.

Population theory is part of the grand tradition of political economy. In times past most clear thinking and courageous vision in this field is attributable to the economists. Lately the economists have, with a few outstanding exceptions, shunned the population problem and left it to be dealt with piecemeal by sociologists, statisticians, and doctors. Again I think that this is more true of this country than other countries, in spite of the relatively much greater crew that mans economics in America, which in other fields has permitted a more complete covering of topics and a greater intensity of work and discussion.

The reluctance of economists to come to grips with the wider aspects of the population problem is, no doubt, related to the general disrepute of classical economy and, at the same time, of broad speculation on social issues. I share in the main the critical motivation for this change of emphasis and of research methods. I should only like to remark in passing that one of the contributory forces, or, at least, one of the phenomena which shelter under the empiricist formula, has been the general and understandable desire to avoid political and ethical conclusions when such conclusions — under the contemporary factual situation and the prevalently dominant social valuations — would take a dangerously radical direction. There is obviously a considerable amount of what I already have termed "escape in facts" in the fact-finding enthusiasm of recent decades.

It should not be overlooked, however, that the deterioration of the grand tradition of political economy in the population problem had begun much earlier. It was already complete in the neoclassical epoch when speculation and general theorizing otherwise reached their highest point. In fact the classical theorists from Adam Smith to John Stuart Mill were not at all confined to pure deduction according to the standards of the marginalists; they were constantly making broad inductions from their experiences of social reality and were not solely or even primarily constrained to deductions from first principles. The modern empirical trend is, therefore, not responsible for the discontinuation of broad population speculation. It had occurred much in advance.

Since John Stuart Mill the science of economics has, in fact, made only one major contribution to this field: the theory of optimum population. This theory, which I am inclined to denote one of the most sterile ideas that ever grew out of our science, was, however, already implied in Mill's postulates. It was early developed in all details by Edgeworth, Sidgwick and Wicksell, was later reinvented by Cannan and his pupils, and was imported to this country after the Great War. Its elaboration has not increased its scientific significance or practical applicability. The theory stands mainly as an excuse for, and also as an actual inhibition of, the proper posing of the problem of the economic effects of population changes. It therefore also invites a liberalistic lack of interest in the political aspects of the population problem so much emphasized in earlier times.

When economics forsook its grand tradition in the study of population the task of visualizing the problem in its broad perspective did not find its performer in any other of the social sciences. The statistician masters a method of research but has not in his thought-ways the tools for effectively gripping the population problem in its wider social and political implications. Raymond Pearl's crude version of the Malthusian natural law of population — his logistic curve — is indeed more of a proof than a disproof of this statement. Hygienists and eugenists are naturally restricted to the biological aspects of the problem. These aspects are tremendously important, but society is not an organism. Sociologists should be the natural heirs of the grand tradition. In this country, the only one where sociology has developed into a broadly ramifying social science, its tradition is restricted, however, by a basic individualistic philosophy. Society becomes in its hands either a rather static structure for the life of individuals or a process of changes and "adjustments" in a continuum from some "balance," or even "harmony," through "disturbances" to some new "balance." In both cases institutions are frequently endowed with teleological "functions" without any explicitly stated assumptions of *telos*. The political premises are constantly pressed underground. The result is that sociology is emasculated so far as its capacity to deal with socio-political problems is concerned. Induced changes have scarcely any other place in this scientific structure than under "adjustments," a conception belonging to its inherited liberalist metaphysics, which constantly tends to restrict induced changes to changes of elements in relation to the system; changes of the "system" are usually not conceived of at all. American sociology won its emancipation as a science by shaking off the influence of preachers and reformers; what it preserved of practical interests followed the intentions of the social workers with their natural concentration on individualized case work and their professional blinders as far as the wider implications are concerned. In general it has neither the tradition nor the ambition even to pose socio-political problems rationally. Political science, finally, must find the population problem rather out of its grasp, since it is concerned more with the forms of politics than its content.

In this situation the task of stating the population problem in its relation to public and individual interests is without a performer — unless the economists again take up the grand tradition. As a further excuse for this book I want to add more particularly the following. We are acquainted with many facts. Population statistics are augmented every year. The psychologist and the sociologist are on the verge of embarking upon more decisive research on the individual motivation, if not the social causation, of the limitation of the modern family. Medical experts are cautiously growing interested in the crucial questions of sterility and fertility, and in the development of the contraceptive technique. The social and political aspect of the population problem, however, is left out or dealt with in a very superficial way. It is this political side of the problem which more than any other just now ought to have a square, rational analysis.

The stereotype, commonly used as a refuge or an excuse by us social scientists, that wise political action requires much more detailed knowledge of the complicated social process than we possess at present, is valid as far as it goes. But it causes us very often to overlook two important truths: one, that political decisions, leading both to action and to inaction, must always be taken, however far behind social fact-finding lags; and the other, that certain general valuations, principles, and main causal relations must be presupposed if detailed research is not to go entirely astray in unintelligent inconsequentials and trifles. These valuations, principles, and main relations should, if possible, be rationally based and systematically coördinated in a social and political philosophy.

With all the excuses piled up behind me, I want in these lectures, for once, to reverse the prudent tactics of most of my fellow economists at the present time. I will venture to take the bull by the horns. I deliberately choose to discuss the population problem frankly as a political problem of social goals and planned political action. And I will not avoid dealing explicitly with its relation to individual ethics. I will also try to be plain and outspoken as to my premises of value — premises which, if hidden, are turned into mere distorting biases, but which, if made explicit, are the very means, and the only means, by which in a rational and scientific manner definite practical conclusions can be inferred from known facts.

II

POPULATION AS A PROBLEM FOR DEMOCRACY

MY MAJOR political premise is the principle of democracy.

This principle does not at present belong to *beati possedentes*. Democracy is forced into combat, with its very existence at stake. If we in the old democracies — and the new ones have already succumbed — mean to preserve our heritage of progress and freedom, we must prove the efficiency of democracy as an institutional frame for social life. The instrumentalities for rational social planning and control must be perfected and engineered; an ever newly created social balance must be achieved by induced changes; the direction of the composite resultant social change must be determined by the majority will of the people; so far as possible this will ought to be determined rationally, i.e., on the basis of the true, sometimes converging and sometimes diverging, interests of the people in different regions and occupations, which interests should, therefore, be ascertained by objective research and the knowledge made available for the broad masses of people.

Strivings in precisely this direction, with varying success, give the tone to daily life in all the democratic countries in northern and western Europe, and in America. Our problems are essentially the same, though circumstantial differences in the kaleidoscope of public interest and discussion are constantly changing and differentiating the picture.

In the present world all major issues, in all fields of government, are fraught with momentous consequences. But to my mind no other factor — not even that of peace or war — is so tremendously fatal for the long-time destinies of democracies as the factor of population. Democracy, not only as a political form but with all its content of civic ideals and human life, must either solve this problem or perish. A development is under way, which is well known by the experts though in most democratic countries it still plays a very minor role in actual politics, but which is bound within a few decades to change the entire basis of social life and, I believe, reshape our social policy.

But are there not, we may ask, certain elements in the population problem which are apt to make democracy apathetic or even averse to the mere idea of having a population policy? If so, there are abundant reasons not to evade the fact of these psychological and political inhibitions but to make them part of our study.

It is probably true that the psychological and political basis for a population policy is weaker in democracies than under dictatorships. Thus, in the ideological basis of democratic society it is deeply inherent that the people are sovereign, that the private individual and his aims have a primacy over the state and its strivings, and that, further, in the nation quality counts for more than quantity. Imperialistic nationalism is naturally ready to accept and preach the value of quantity of population, but an aggressive expansionist policy is the very denial of democracy, since the principle both of a ruling class and a ruling nation means oligarchy.

These very broad generalizations have been presented merely as preliminary rationalizations in terms of national policy for those population inhibitions in democracies of which everyone who has been working in the field is well aware. The question is, however: How stable are these inhibitions? Do they represent more than an initial difficulty, like many other elements of the inertia that makes democracy inherently a more slowly moving political mechanism than the ruled totalitarian countries? How will they react when the population situation is explicitly known to endanger the continuation of a nation and a culture?

An intellectualist like myself must pursue the question one step further and ask for the *rationale* in the problem: Do there exist for the ordinary citizens of a democratic, nonimperialistic country rational reasons to worry about the development of population? By "rational reasons" I mean reasons which are based on an evaluation of the different sorts of consequences of the alternative possibilities in population development — the evaluation to be arrived at by weighing these effects by the social valuations and political attitudes prevalent in democratic society. And we must further ask, in the event that such reasons are found, what direction they indicate as preferable for population development to take.

As politics in a democracy is ultimately based on the will of the citizens, the inquiry must be further pursued: How in actual experience do people making up public opinion react to the prospects in the matter of population development when once we have succeeded in making them aware of its course? Are they apt to look upon an approaching decline in population with alarm, or will they remain indifferent? How are people's opinions in the population problem related to and associated with their political attitudes in other respects, their religious ideas, their social class, their income, etc.? Furthermore, what is the relationship of people's political attitudes toward the population problem and their personal attitudes as builders of families and bearers of children? In a democracy the possibilities of gathering supporters about a population policy, as well as the success and efficiency of the measures embraced in such a policy, depend on the answers of these closely related questions. Again it must be inquired: What relations are there between people's population attitudes and their sex, age, the number of children in the family in which they were born, and the number in the family which they themselves have begotten? Since these characteristics of a population are changing considerably as a result of the very development of population, these last questions are of the utmost importance for an understanding of the dynamics of the political problem.

From this we are brought to the third group of questions. Assuming for the sake of the argument that a positive population policy can be vindicated, what measures can be taken to influence people's behavior as to marrying and breeding children? In a democracy this question has the following import: By what means can the composite resultant of people's political attitudes be brought to influence their own private attitudes? — and, we must add, do this without intruding upon personal liberty and other basic norms of democracy.

For it is clear at the outset that, even if the

initial inhibitions in a democratic culture against a population policy *per se* can be overcome under the pressure of the actual tendency of population development and of a wide popular knowledge of it and its implications, these same inhibitions will nevertheless be of tremendous importance in narrowly restricting the methods which are to be utilized for the purpose. The bearing of those inhibitions might be changed from prejudicing a goal to merely forbidding certain means; but the inhibitions as such are essential for democracy and cannot be given up except by forsaking democracy. They contain its basic social values and political principles. An analysis of the restrictions under which population policy must work in a democracy is thus of primary importance in our problem.

The specific realm of interference on the part of modern democratic society, for which there is characteristically no established *terminus technicus* in the English language but which I will denote as social policy, stands out as embracing the chief means of arriving at a democratic population policy. By social policy I mean the whole complex of political measures taken to enhance the material and spiritual well-being of the broad masses of a population. I will raise the question: Does the development of population constitute an argument for enlarging and redirecting social policy? If such is the case, what are the principles for remolding a rational social policy to serve the ends of population policy as well?

By stating these questions I have, though very broadly, delimited the field of these lectures. It is thus not my intention to deal exhaustively and independently, with either the population problem, standing alone, or social policy, standing alone. I do not expect to go into statistical detail on the question of the development of population, either in the world as a whole or in individual countries. As to the tendencies of population development, a few broad generalizations will constitute the total of my remarks. Nor shall I attempt to be at all complete in my treatment of the large and heterogeneous complex of political interferences in economic and social life which I group under the term social policy.[1] The subject of these lectures is rather the *re-*

[1] For an exhaustive analysis of this problem see Alva Myrdal's forthcoming book.

lation between the population problem and social policy, or, to state it even more definitely, *the political element in the population problem.* Even so delimited, the scope is immense; and no elaboration is needed to make it clear that only a broad overview will be possible. The writer will be satisfied if, within this narrow space, he succeeds only in stating open problems and formulating some broad hypotheses.

Some of the simplifications underlying my discussion should be explicitly stated. First, I am not touching upon international implications and complications, but am adhering entirely to the associations of the population problem with a nation's domestic policy. I am thus keeping the issue of a democratic population policy entirely clear of even the possibility of imperialistic interests. Second, I am assuming a population without any consciousness of racial differences within its stock, and thus without even the possibility of applying value differentials to the propagation of various social groups of the people. I am quite aware that I am thereby excluding many of the most ramifying implications of the political population problem, not least in this country, and, therefore, also limiting the general validity of some of the conclusions. But I believe it well worth while to study such a simplified laboratory case first. Third, I am restricting my study to contemporary industrialized western civilization. As I have already pointed out I am, fourth, assuming a democratic system of government.

III

THE LABORATORY

FOR A NUMBER of reasons I shall use Sweden as my point of reference in this analysis. What I shall have to say will not be based merely on bookish material, reflection, and speculation, for Sweden has become, during the last few years, an experimental laboratory for the theories I shall posit.

In the first chapter the great secular swings of intelligent opinion on the population problem were set forth and the relation of these swings to changing rates of propagation was pointed out. Just as during the course of history, different rates of procreation have given a quite different political content to the population problem in different periods, so the population problem has a quite different political content in different cultures and different countries even at the present time.

There is thus no single political theory by which the population problem may be generally treated. For example, the population problem simply is not the same problem in the East as in the West. And if — as I do not believe probable — the absorptive capacity of American industry should cease for a long period of time, the population problem of the impoverished backward regions in the South, in the mountain districts, and in the cut-over areas in the Lake states in the north of this country, left in partial isolation, would be much more like the problem as it presents itself in southern and eastern Asia, and this would not allow its incorporation in a unified statement of an American population problem.

In countries having a western civilization and being in a process of continuous industrialization — short of intermediary and minor setbacks — the political aspect of the population problem is nevertheless sufficiently uniform to permit a fairly general and uniform treatment. In all these countries the trend of fertility, by and large, has for a long time been uninterruptedly downward. In northern and western Europe for a considerable number of years the rate of fertility has been far below the level at which population just reproduces itself; the populations of these countries will soon reach the peak and then begin to decrease. The situation in these countries seems, upon close study of statistics and underlying sociological processes, only to foreshadow a population trend which in years or decades will take place similarly in other countries. It is true that in the United States the net reproduction index for the population as a whole — using the term in the meaning Kuczynski has given it — still stands at a point not far from the level where the population continues completely to reproduce itself. But the fertility rate steadily tends to decrease.

In spite of the big differences in the birth rate of countries like Sweden, Holland, England, and the United States — differences which, as is recognized, stand out even more markedly if a comparison be made between different geographical districts and social classes within each of these lands considered as a unit — the tendency in the direction of a declining reproduction rate constitutes a similar problem in all of these countries. In the dynamics of population these differences typically may be characterized as differentiated merely by a time lag: certain countries, and in these certain social groups, find themselves ten and twenty years in the van of the tendency. It must, therefore, I think, be of universal interest for all of these cultures to study the conditions in the countries where the tendency has gone furthest. Now Sweden, which I shall use to a certain extent as the point of reference in my general analysis, is such a country. Sweden has for a long time occupied the lowest place, or one of the next to the lowest places, among all nations in the matter of birth rate and level of net reproduction.

This place of honor has nevertheless been achieved, from a historical point of view, only rather recently and as the result of a quick development. In Sweden the birth rate per thousand, which during the whole nineteenth century and even further back had kept just above 30 per thousand, did not begin to fall until the beginning of the eighties. At first the decline was very slow indeed. In 1900 it was down only to 27 per thousand; the actual number of children born did not begin to fall before the years preceding the Great War. Then the movement gained momentum and — except for the mysterious upward movement in 1920–21, experienced in Sweden as in all western lands — it attained a pace which became more and more rapid. Sweden fell below the line of 100 per cent net reproduction in 1925, and is now down to a net reproduction figure under 75 per cent. In 1934 the crude birth rate sank to a low of 13.68 per thousand. At about this point the figures have lingered during the last few years.

It will now be interesting to ask the following question. When in a country like Sweden reproduction has reached this very low level — where the potential stock of the population diminishes to a half in little more than two generations — does this level represent a bottom or will the fall in fertility continue? A forecast of the trend is naturally one of the most difficult tasks to embark upon. When I nevertheless venture to undertake it, I do it with all the natural reservations for the unpredictable.

On the whole, the prospects are for a continued, and very considerable, fall in reproduction. The differences in fertility between different districts and social classes are broad. In towns the net reproduction is down to about 50 per cent; in Stockholm and some other cities the figure is below 40 per cent. In rural areas as a whole the net reproduction is still around 90 per cent; in the agricultural districts it stands over 100 per cent. In the northern provinces of Sweden the birth rate is at the same level as for the whole country before the war, corresponding to a net reproduction of 120–130 per cent and in some districts even more. A breakdown of families according to income groups and social status shows — except for Stockholm and some other cities with a very low level of average reproduction — in general a strong negative correlation between income and social status, on the one hand, and number of children, on the other. Thus, the majority of families with a great number of children are concentrated in the lower income brackets.

This situation is a highly unstable one, for no cross-sectional check of positions during a dynamic process ever does give permanent relations. The industrialization and urbanization of the nation, for example, have not come to a standstill by far but continue rapidly on two frontiers. First, there is a strong migration going on from rural to urban districts and from agricultural to industrial and commercial occupations, thus gradually diminishing the portion of the population in those districts and occupations where fertility has been high. The agricultural population is still over a third of the total population, and this shift has not reached its final limits. Secondly, urban culture is continually making strong impacts on the residual rural culture, a process which has no limit other than the approach to a unified urban national culture. The old rural folk society is rapidly loosing its moorings. The Scandinavian farmer has to apply a capitalistic technique and a collectivistic organizational life which does not harmonize with the old rural folkways; religion is also losing its hold upon his soul, and he seeks and acquires for his children the educational opportunities of urban children.

At the same time the rapid and general rise of the standard of living, in the country as well as in cities, enhanced for the poorest classes by a gradually accomplished system of social security and other distributional reforms, is diminishing all the time that portion of the nation which is actually poverty-stricken, and which still is responsible for most of the families with the many children.

As a consequence of these unidirectional social changes the general tendency, clearly visible when the statistical figures are analyzed in detail, is, and has been for many years, that births are falling more rapidly in the districts and the social classes where the rate is high. In these districts and classes fertility falls even during years when it is temporarily stationary or rising in the other districts and classes. A leveling off of the big differences is under way. This leveling process goes downward. The high rates that still prevail in some districts and some classes are mainly to be judged as a phenomenon of social lag in a dynamic development.

For Sweden we know pretty surely that involuntary sterility and spontaneous abortion have not been increasing during the last two generations comprising the modern trend of decreasing fertility. The direct cause of the fall in fertility is, therefore, increasing birth control. The birth figures show, furthermore, that at present birth control of some sort or other, and with varying degrees of efficiency, is being exercised in almost all marriages, except the sterile ones and the comparatively few marriages with a biblical number of children. Partly by inference from the statistics of differential fertility and from the statistics of the sales of contraceptives, and partly from direct investigations, we know further, however, that the methods applied are mostly not very reliable. Even the urban middle classes seem to rely to a surprisingly great extent on *coitus interruptus*. The fall in fertility up to now is thus not to a considerable degree to be explained by the spread of technical means of contraception. But we can at the same time ascertain that the practice of more efficient birth control methods is rapidly spreading from year to year. This factor by itself also gives countenance to the forecast that we have not yet seen the bottom of the falling curve of fertility in Sweden.

That there is still much room for improved birth control even in Sweden with its already exceptionally low fertility rate is further indicated by the high illegitimacy rate. Around one-seventh of all births occur out of wedlock; this proportion is now declining. Everyone with any social experience knows that not only most of these illegitimate births but also a very large portion of the births within marriages are the consequence not of a desire for parenthood but simply of faulty contraceptive technique. The parents, in the common phrase, are merely the victims of bad luck. Perhaps a third, perhaps even half of all births in Sweden are in this sense "undesired"; these births will decrease from year to year as a consequence of the spread of a more reliable contraceptive technique. I would like to emphasize the point that there is very much room for such an expansion of effective birth control even in a city like Stockholm, where the aggregate net reproduction is down nearly to a third and where in the middle and upper classes, as the late Dr. Edin has shown, there has been a positive correlation between marital fertility, on the one hand, and social and economic status, on the other.

An indirect proof, or at least a strong indication, of this pessimistic prognosis is contained in the birth figures for the very last years. There has been a great increase in the number of marriages (from 6.75 per thousand in 1932 to 8.67 in 1937 and 9.01 in 1938), the explanation being, first and most important, changes in the age distribution favoring the age classes with the higher marriage expectancy, and, second, the rising economic tide which in 1937 had brought the index of industrial production 50 per cent above its level in 1929. With more marriages there naturally follows a certain number of extra births; and it should be indicated that in the present situation the rise in marriages ought to have a proportionately greater effect upon the average birth rate, since, as an effect of falling fertility, first-born children now constitute a greater proportion than before of all children born. The rising boom ever since 1934, which among other results has increased the sum of real wages by more than a third (chiefly by reducing unemployment and part-time work), must *per se* imply a tendency toward raising the birth rate even within the older marriages. In spite of these two strong forces — the abnormally large number of persons attaining marriageable age and marrying, and the economic boom — the birth rate per thousand has increased very slightly (13.71 in 1933; 13.68 in 1934; 13.76 in 1935; 14.17 in 1936; 14.33 in 1937; and 14.85 in 1938). These forces, the transitoriness of which is obvious even without detailed comment, have only been strong enough approximately — and of course only temporarily — to balance the trend, which seems continually to point downward.

The conclusion is that the reproduction of the Swedish population, here used as a point of reference, which is already about 25 per cent under the parity level, in all probability, unless very powerful measures are devised and successfully applied within the near future, will fall to a level still lower than that to which it has already sunk. I do not believe we ought to be surprised if the population should attain its maximum and start to fall within the next ten years, and if the net reproduction figure should drop to 50 per cent, which would mean that the potential stock of Swedish population would be diminished by half in one generation. I have in this connection supposed that no sufficiently strong population policy can be introduced, or could, within a short period, have sufficient success to stem the tide.

These conclusions from direct studies of the factors in the dynamics of the population mechanism are strengthened if one addresses himself to a closer analysis of the distribution of families in different size categories, which correspond to the different reproduction rates. Such a statistical study, which I unfortunately cannot refer to in detail, gives the following chief conclusion: If it be desired to raise the net reproduction rate from the present 70–75 per cent, to 100 per cent, then three things must happen: first, the number of marriages resulting in less than three children must be reduced from the present figure of approximately half of all marriages to one-third of all marriages; second, the majority of the remaining two-thirds of all marriages must result in more than three children; third, if age-corrected nuptiality should not permanently increase, then a great number of this majority of two-thirds would have to have five children. All of which quite plainly means that not only the "two-child system" of the Neo-Malthusian propaganda but even a "three-child system" is incompatible with keeping a population constant. In judging the applicability to other countries of these results of our research, it must be borne in mind that on the one hand the marriage rate in Sweden is fairly low, but that on the other hand the illegitimate birth rate is high and the death rate unusually low.

During recent years there have been carried out in Sweden very intensive statistical studies of the level of living in families of different sizes. This research in differential family standards has given quantitative precision to the common-sense opinion that the level of living in families in general (although high and fairly even when compared with the levels reached in most other countries) is very low even in Sweden when judged by commonly accepted standards of health and decency; and that, more particularly, having children, beginning with the first child but especially with a larger number of children, constitutes a most powerful downward pressure upon the standard of living. If, now, the result of this research, where we have actually been measuring the "real cost" of an additional child, be juxtaposed with the calculations in regard to the change in distribution of families in the size categories necessary to maintain a stationary population, then it is difficult to avoid the two following important conclusions: (1) that a reproduction rate sufficient to actually increase the population is an unreasonable and impossible goal for a population policy in a land like Sweden, and I think generally in the western world, a stationary population constituting the maximum possibility even with the strongest population policy; (2) that, unless such a policy is successfully applied, a continued marked decline of fertility in marriages is the probable outcome of future development. This analysis of the underlying causal factors thus only strengthens the conclusions already reached by the statistical analysis of the dynamics of the population mechanism as such.

We must here remember the democratic structure of a country like Sweden, with democratic principles penetrating deeply the whole outlook on life, and, further, the intensive popular education spreading, with the support of the state, hygienic and cultural ideals in regard to what constitutes a decent standard of living, a standard which for the majority of families is clearly incompatible with having and rearing a normal number of children. In the whole cultural sphere of western democracies our policy is, and must continue to be, constantly to keep the ideals of a decent standard far in front of actual possibilities — *if* extreme birth control is not to be the assumption. When I state this dilemma it is not merely a broad generalization of mine but can be, and has been, demonstrated and proved by penetrating statistical research carried out during recent years on the standard of living in Swedish families of different sizes. I refer specifically to the works of Mr. Richard Sterner of the Swedish Social Board.

To achieve a fertility rate sufficient to maintain population, the majority of non-sterile marriages must produce four children. Ordinary citizens making up the bulk of every nation — the workers, farmers, clerks, and all the others whose means are small — these ordinary citizens, we say, will certainly be privately inclined, from mere prudence and sense of responsibility, not to follow such a population policy unless vast distributional reforms in the interest of families with children are enacted, reforms so radical that public opinion at present is certainly not prepared to accept more than a small fraction of them at most. The ordinary person will be inclined, on the contrary, to restrict the number of his children still more. It is to be concluded, therefore, that the declining trend in the fertility rate will in all probability continue.

I have chosen to use Sweden as a point of reference in these lectures, first, for the natural reason that Sweden is the part of the world where I am most thoroughly acquainted not only with the statistical material but also with the less tangible social realities behind such quantitative data. Furthermore, the Swedes have gone exceptionally far in applying rational birth control; if, therefore, as I assume, the process we are studying has a common pattern, it must be of interest to study a population which is in the front in this process. From the political aspect, particularly, Sweden is a most useful background; as I will indicate in the next chapter the population process there has instigated a crisis of opinion.

In utilizing Sweden as my population laboratory, I believe that I should insert a few observations in order that the milieu of the experiment may be sufficiently defined.

Quite generally it may be said that there are a number of elements in the Swedish cultural situation which make it possible to study our present problem — population in democratic politics — in a very pure form and released from a number of complications, which must be of considerable advantage in the first general approach. For one thing, there are in Sweden practically no race differences explicit in the popular mind and, consequently, none of the important ramifying effects on the whole cultural situation, and especially on the political outlook on population, which, as we well know, are apt to go together with consciousness of race differences. The same is true as to religion. The country has an Evangelical Lutheran state church, with the clergy part of the civil service, but the population is secularized to an unusually high degree and not very religious. There is, naturally, absolute religious freedom, but the sects are even more inconsequential. In the Swedish situation there is, further, no temptation, nor even a possibility, to introduce imperialistic ambitions into the question. The country has enjoyed peace for much more than one hundred years, and the whole people lost the ability to think in realistic terms of itself as involved in a war. For generations its main principle of foreign policy has been to keep out of foreign policy.

Public education is moderately high, which means that there is a stronger and quicker response to new ideas than in most countries. The general public reads books and is apt to pursue quite complicated arguments. Swedish culture has, on the whole, a strongly rationalistic and technical slant. Because of the inherited decentralization of administration and politics, most conspicuous in local self-government, a greater portion of the people than in perhaps any other land takes an active part in government, not only as voters but also as elected representatives and as officeholders of one sort or another. Large civic organizations function in the same way to activize democratic citizenship: the trade union movement, which embraces almost 100 per cent of Swedish labor; the consumers' coöperatives, taking care of a quarter of the whole retail trade in foodstuffs and a tenth of this trade as a whole; the producers' coöperatives, and other similar institutions. This means that the population, in spite of a highly developed individualism, has perhaps a stronger sense of collective participation in social affairs, and a greater feeling of responsibility for the well-being of the whole country, than populations of other countries can possess.

This goes together with a practically uncorrupted state in politics and administration. There is a considerable amount of coöperation in politics between the different parties. The stable power situation forces the conservatives to be comparatively radical, and the radicals to behave conservatively. For many years the country has been governed by a Social Democratic government: the Socialists actually got a majority of the votes at the election in 1936, and now both chambers of Parliament have a Social Democratic basis. The farmers actively support the Social Democratic government, and since 1936 have had three posts in the Cabinet, strengthening its stable power basis. It is a long time since the prospect of such a development has disconcerted business and finance very much. Underneath all public attitudes there exists a quiet, conservative temperament embracing great and genuine scepticism. The people have constantly shown that they are in an unusually marked degree not susceptible to panic. The generally secure situation has given men the feeling that "everything will be all right" if proper public measures are taken.

Economically and socially, the country is in a high degree a "new country." In the 1870's three-fourths of the population was agricultural. Today the agricultural population is not much more than one-third of the total. Industrialization came late but developed apace. Since we remained out of the war, our prosperity, relatively speaking, was less affected than elsewhere in Europe. The terms of international trade during the post-war period, together with other elements in our business situation, permitted thereafter a more progressive economic development than in most other countries. The depression of 1929–33 did not strike as hard in Sweden as it did in the majority of other lands. Recovery was swift and strong; as early as 1934 Sweden was well on the way to a new period of prosperity. Sweden practically skipped the depression of 1937–38. Industrial production reached in 1937 a level 50 per cent higher than the pre-depression peak of 1929, which, in its turn, was 50 per cent higher than the level of 1920.[1]

[1] The reader who finds this sketch of the laboratory milieu too incomplete is referred to two articles by the present author in the *Survey Graphic* of May and June 1939, where some of the points are elaborated.

IV

THE CRISIS OF OPINION

I HAVE pointed out that in Sweden the net reproduction rate has already fallen to less than three-fourths of that necessary to maintain a stationary population balance. I have hinted at certain reasons on the basis of which I regard it as probable that the tendency will be toward a still greater disequilibrium between births and deaths in the near future. Since I am not able here to extend my observations to all western civilization, I have confined myself to Sweden as a population laboratory. I regard the differences between different countries within western society as of the same kind as the differences between different districts and social classes in one of the countries. Naturally I perceive full well that the various causal phenomena I have touched upon in regard to Sweden have very different proportions in different lands. I nevertheless believe that, taken together, and viewed in a long-range perspective, they must indicate approximately the same final result: a decline in a fertility rate to a point very far below the rate which must be maintained if a population is not to vanish.

My thesis in this chapter is the following. This development in population must sooner or later unleash in western society an ideological crisis in popular attitudes toward the population question. The dispassionate and mostly evasive discussion of scientists, which is going on in all our countries and has been going on for decades, the exertions of the dictatorships, and the diffusive endeavors which have been brought into play even in some of the democratic countries, are mere harbingers of the furious clash of opinion which soon must make itself felt.

In reality it is surprising that this ideological crisis has not already waxed to its full strength. In England, for example, which has quite as serious a population situation as Sweden in view of the decimated war generation of men and the sharply shrunken generation of children from the war years, phenomena which are, of course, not paralleled in Sweden, the fact that the population problem has not as yet aroused greater political attention is far from natural, and something which very much needs to be explained.

By way of making such an explanation I would like tentatively to submit a few general remarks. For one thing, the type of persons making liberal opinion articulate in Anglo-Saxon as in northern countries is still to a very great extent dominated by Neo-Malthusianism. As long as progressives are forced to struggle against strong conservative social conventions — and even legal restrictions — in order to spread birth control among the poorer classes and among exhausted mothers, the Neo-Malthusian ideology will retain a vigor which it otherwise long ago would have lost. A social doctrine, like a religion, quite generally thrives on persecution, and thus the opposition to Neo-Malthusianism strengthens and conserves instead of weakening it. At all events, this is true to the extent that the progressives at least are not yet prepared to take the initiative in a positive population policy. But neither will the conservatives take a strong initiative, inasmuch as they must have certain premonitions that a positive population policy in modern society would mean social reforms and be a heavy drain upon the public treasury.

The circumstance that the dictatorships happen to be very articulate in their population policy also, in a democratic country like England, engenders aversion for every attempt to enunciate a positive population policy, and further strengthens Neo-Malthusianism. The hard times which in England have prevailed pretty continuously since the war, and the great amount of unemployment, moreover, capture public attention, as of more immediate importance. According to old tradition, and without much reflection, unemployment is linked with the somewhat obscure concept of "overpopulation," and it is thus being urged that a diminution of population is desirable from the economic point of view. This latter theory, which I regard as more than questionable,[1] is not only entertained by "the man in the street," but also until lately by economists, at least as far as their thought is represented in the press available for the general public.

[1] See below in Chapter VI.

Finally the fear-breeding international situation in recent years has aroused such intense attention that there is not much space left in the minds of people for such a "new" and, in a way, distant problem as the question of population in its modern form.

For America some of the above remarks have a similar bearing. But, above all, the average reproduction rate, in spite of the definitely downward trend, is still at a rather high level compared with northern Europe and there is felt to be no very immediate danger of population decline. Until recently, moreover, the country has experienced immigration on a huge scale. Public discussion over immigration barriers is only of yesterday and is still burning under the surface. The great majority favoring these barriers is focusing its interest upon the defense of wages and standards for the native population; they are naturally not very susceptible to the idea that there might be danger in a check in the growth of the American population. Their opponents, if they should be swayed by such a suspicion, are inclined to see in immigration the most natural remedy.

There are, furthermore, a great many elements in American society tending to complicate, confuse, and emotionally disturb a general discussion of population. One such element is, naturally, the racial and cultural cleavages within this composite nation. Another factor, which generally blocks the way for broad ideological discussion of political issues, is the lack of political parties organized upon diverging ideals and class interests, and, more broadly, the particular effects of the fragmentation of the lower social strata and some other peculiarities in American social development in inhibiting the social, economic, and political mass movements of other democratic countries. A third general factor is the extraordinarily strong impact of church and religion in America. From the point of view of the present problem, specifically, the fundamentalist character of Protestant religion in some of the regions where fertility is highest is of importance, as is also the grip of the Catholic Church over very large groups of poor families in northern cities.

During the last decade the stagnation of economic development in America and the consequent struggles and changes in the sphere of economic policy have absorbed public interest. This stagnation has also, as is usually not observed on either side in the fights going on, distorted the rational perspective on practically all social problems. Perhaps the most disheartening general effect of a prolonged economic stagnation is that by the logic of emergency practically all ordinary social problems take on a perverted appearance. When the economic system is permanently working on a level far under its capacity, the normal and prudent questions of balance in the location of resources lose most of their interest; the resources are not scarce, they are free, and the only thing that matters is to get the system working. When public spending is getting an independent value as "compensatory" or "stimulating," the normal problems of in what direction to spend and under what permanent fiscal structure are relegated to second rank. When full employment cannot be secured for the workers a most extraordinary problem arises of how to "share" employment by shortening weekly hours far below what is rationally motivated by reasons of efficiency of production and maximum standard of well-being for the workers. When industry cannot absorb the increasing rural surplus population the practical worry is how to establish subsistence farming, even if the level of living procured in this way will not reach over a substandard. In this perverted world of stagnation economics there is, of course, no place for a rational long-range discussion of the population problem otherwise than grossly disfigured in the same manner. But stagnation cannot be everlasting in America. Either the problem of full employment will be solved by preserving the essentials of democracy and free enterprise, or this institutional frame will be transformed, for no political system can long sustain economic stagnation. Of these two alternatives I want to believe in the first one. The second would, of course, beg my question entirely, first in regard to this country and, consequently, I am afraid, for the whole western world.

As a general explanation of the lag of public interest and public opinion in population questions, reference must finally be made to the fact that the figures for total population, and also most economic effects, follow after the initial changes in reproduction rate at a space of twenty to forty years. The very idea of true net reproduction seems to be one of the most difficult social relations for the general public which makes up the basis for political discussion in a democratic country to grasp. The opinion lag is, naturally, a function both of the general educational level in social questions in a country and also of the amount and efficiency of the educational forces applied to the problem of population.

These cursory remarks by way of explaining the relative indifference in the great Anglo-Saxon democracies toward the political population problem might be wrong without endangering my central thesis in the present stage of the argument. Assume, as I do, that the fertility trend is steadily downward. Sooner or later, then, an ideological crisis in the population problem will emerge. That the crisis has been postponed by these or other factors means only that the latent explosive power concealed within the decline of reproduction is accumulating, and that the crisis, when once it comes, will be all the more violent.

In the long range, as I anticipate, this ideological crisis will have revolutionary effects upon all social policy and upon men's attitudes toward all sorts of human problems. After this crisis, which must occur in western Europe within the next few decades but in America may be considerably deferred if the fall in fertility is not very rapid, the population problem will come to dominate all social life.

It seems to be of considerable interest to inquire further how this impending crisis will appear and what it will bring in its track. Let me return again to Sweden. I am fully conscious that this small country, which contains fewer persons than some large cities in other lands, is not *per se* a significant factor in world development. I am using Swedish material only to construct a sort of case study. Sweden may well serve as a scientific laboratory for political studies of the population problem. For during recent years a clash of opinion in relation to that problem has taken place in Sweden which, for a number of reasons, I believe, will soon have its counterpart in other democratic countries. The study of population policy which has been made in Sweden — in part the cause and in part the result of this clash of opinion — probably has to a marked degree a general significance for democratic western civilization.

In Sweden the same great secular currents of ideas in the field of population theory have been experienced that have been experienced in the western world at large. Earlier Swedish population discussion, like Swedish economic development and Swedish economic thinking in general, came, however, rather late, compared with the English development. Swedish writings on population are of almost no general interest until late in the seventies of the last century, when Knut Wicksell made Neo-Malthusianism articulate in Sweden too. It was, in fact, an interest in the population problem which originally turned Wicksell's interest toward economics, and in addition to his very important work in monetary and central economic theory, he always had his mind deeply engaged with the population issue. He developed early a population optimum theory of the type which later was proposed by Professor Cannan and others, and which has been fashionable in America since the war. Wicksell used this theory to expound in a vague and general way the desirability of a smaller population in Sweden.

Parallel to the declining birth rate, which I have already discussed in the preceding chapter, the Neo-Malthusian ideas won acceptance not only in the labor movement and in liberal circles but much more widely. It was very generally agreed that decreasing fertility was an index of high culture, and a strong power for raising the standard of living.

It is inherent in the nature of the thing, however, that such a development of population sooner or later had to bring on a crisis, if not a panic, in popular attitudes toward the population question. This crisis came to Sweden in the fall of 1934, after an accumulation of the normal downward trend in fertility and the effects of the economic depression had resulted in a severely accelerated decline in the birth rate which marked the year 1933 with a birth rate of 13.79. The recovery from the economic crisis, then well under way, at the same time allowed public interest to be given to other than economic crisis problems. The spark which touched off the 1934 fireworks was a book which, though a rather heavy sociological treatise of four hundred pages, was very widely circulated in all social classes. The population situation immediately began to be discussed intensively in the press and on the radio; a flood of pamphlets appeared, and the subject shortly was brought to the floor of Parliament and debated by all political parties. A Royal Commission on the Swedish population problem was set to work in the spring of 1935 — soon followed, incidentally, by the establishment of a similar commission in Denmark and later in Finland. The Swedish Commission produced seventeen reports, which embrace detailed plans for large reforms to improve the economic situation of families with children. The majority of these proposals have been adopted by the Cabinet and enacted by Parliament. The 1937 session of the Swedish Parliament came to be called "the mothers and babies session."

Meanwhile a general discussion has been uninterruptedly carried on in newspapers and elsewhere. The question has been studied and debated in adult education groups. In a short space of time popular attitudes changed immensely. A study of the language should reveal that a great number of words, now used by the general public without a thought of their newness, were actually created or at least introduced into the Swedish language in the fall of 1934. This is only to indicate the extent to which public discussion has embraced new thoughts which earlier did not press for expression.

I should like to predict, however, that there will soon be a temporary abatement in the lively interest in the population problem in Sweden. Psychologically, an intense interest is usually followed by a reaction of apathy. The average citizen will, further, feel relieved from the pressure of the problem simply because far-reaching reforms, proposed by the Population Commission, are being discussed and gradually set in operation. Because of the abnormal age distribution, moreover, the population will continue to increase, although very slowly, for some years still. The general public will never quite grasp — or at least not comfortably believe — the statistician's analysis of true reproduction. The crude birth rate, furthermore, has temporarily paused in its decline, because of the present abnormal age distribution and the strong boom of the last few years. The crude marriage rate is actually increasing very considerably as a result of the same causes. The unsophisticated person — the most important entity in public opinion in any country — will think, therefore, that the fall in reproduction has stopped and is turning. The reasons why he is wrong I have already briefly summed up in the preceding chapter.

It is certainly not for me to question the reforms now being inaugurated in Sweden. They are radical enough when viewed in comparison with old conventions; many of the reforms now part of practical policy in Sweden, as for instance the free school luncheon for all children without needs or means tests, two or three years ago were considered quite irresponsible Utopian ideas, which certainly neither the respectable expert nor the practical politician was prepared to support. Nevertheless these reforms are rather futile compared with the thorough reconstruction of the economic basis for the institution of the family, which in a country like Sweden is necessary if the family is to be rescued from sterility and the population kept from vanishing.

The population question will, therefore, become a burning one in Sweden again, probably during the upswing after the next big depression, or — it may be — after the next world war, if Sweden persists as an independent democracy. The cyclical fall of fertility will then again have accentuated the falling trend — just as it did in 1934, and in the same way as at the present time a cyclical rise in births accompanying the economic boom has counterbalanced it — and thus the fall will bring the birth rate down to a new and still more alarming minimum. At about the same time the figure for total population will probably reach its peak and the actual decline of population slowly set in. That will mean very much to the ordinary citizen, who has never quite trusted our learned discussions of abnormal age distribution and related phenomena, but who now will acquire all our wisdom at once. At the same time the pressure of the old-age groups will begin to be felt increasingly, and the building industry will begin to feel more severely the effects of the approaching cessation in the rise of the number of families. Similarly, the effects of the changes in age distribution will cause difficulties in the labor supply in agriculture and other important sectors of the national economy.

We will then see a revival of the population question. This revival will be permanent, and thereafter the population question will dominate our whole economic and social policy for the entire future.

V

PEOPLE'S OPINIONS

A CRISIS of opinion of the type described in the previous chapter has its dynamic force in an anxiety among the population for the reproduction of the nation. Its strength can be roughly apprehended from the willingness, arising from this force, to endure the fiscal burden of quite a vigorously expanded family social reform activity. The question arises: Why, in pure fact, has the ordinary Swedish citizen become anxious about population developments? What interest does he feel in insuring the survival of the nation? Why shouldn't he keep quiet and aloof, attend to his own business, and let the Swedish population decline?

The question can be answered in two different ways. One answer concerns the *rationale* of the problem and states the reasons he should have as an individual and a citizen, provided he knew his interests and faced them squarely. To provide such an answer constitutes the primary duty of social science in a democracy. The object is then to rationalize the political problem facing the citizen by an analysis of the effects which population development will have and by an evaluation of these effects in terms of the citizen's basic ideals and interests. It is true that science cannot determine these ultimate valuations, which, furthermore, are different in different groups; but it can, if they are given, and after having established the facts, point out how rational opinions may be based upon these valuations and the relevant factual data. This problem will be taken up in the next chapter.

Scientific deliberation after this pattern, however, does not dominate public opinion in any country directly and exclusively, though the higher the educational level of people, the more it tends to do so. Of primary importance in the political problem therefore is another version of our question: How, in actual experience, do ordinary citizens form their political attitudes in this problem? This variation of the question raises a problem of sociological observation as to how political opinions are molded and how they are related to the actual social situations of citizens and to their life experiences. Recently developed methods of registering and analyzing attitudes and opinions have here their field. For an analysis of the course of political developments in a democratic country this latter problem is of primary significance.

Returning again to my point of reference, Sweden, I should deem it of the highest importance to analyze the dynamics of population opinion in that country during recent years. It should be of importance, not merely with respect to Sweden, but quite generally with respect to western democracies, for the Swedish "man in the street" is probably not very dissimilar to the English or American, and, in so far as he is different, even the differences should be illuminating.

A realistic study in the dynamics of population opinion is not at all impossible to carry out. My wife and I have arranged a collection of more than ten thousand newspaper clippings from the autumn of 1934 onwards, together with hundreds of pamphlets and more elaborate periodical articles; we have also preserved thousands of letters from compatriots whose reflections upon population policy have been stimulated to such a degree that they have desired to impart to us their views upon the matter. Critically analyzed, and supplemented by direct inquiries, this material should be revealing.

Such organized, scientifically checked research work has not been done. What I will have to say is not based upon systematic research but represents simply a more general, partly intuitive, conception founded upon a cursory inspection of the material mentioned and upon intensive living in the atmosphere of the Swedish population debate for three years. It is humbly presented as hypotheses for better organized research.

At the outset one thing is obvious. A positive attitude in the population problem is unthinkable except on the basis of a kind of psychological *identification of the individual with the people*, the nation conceived of as the collective unit living down the generations. The citizen fears the expiration of the people in the same way, although of course not in the same degree, as he fears his own death.

Psychologically, it is a question of an expanded family sentiment, and thus a mild form of nationalism. When this national *horror vacui*, which of course is very spontaneous and not necessarily founded on reason and consideration, clothes itself in intellectual terms, it can, for instance, assume something like the following form: After all, we in this country are all striving to build up a social and cultural structure of our own, better than the one we inherited. The task of legislation and reforms, all public interests, in fact all sorts of ambitions reaching outside the individual citizen's own threshold would lose most of its urge and, indeed, its meaning were it only a question of administering to the difficulties of a continuous shrinkage of the population.

It is most interesting to note that in this very involved complex of attitudes based on a psychological identification of the individual with the nation, military interests and foreign policy have played practically no role at all in Sweden — or in all Scandinavia — as far as can be ascertained from the popular discussion of the population problem during recent years. Interest in national expansion has been absent. On the other hand, however, it has been widely feared that a rapidly shrinking population, inheriting a rich and roomy country, must attract foreign immigration. There has been the feeling that immigration in modern times, and for a small country in Sweden's geopolitical position, is an affair which probably does not go without international friction. A strong feeling against immigration grew up during the post-war years in all countries — the immigration limitations of the United States are certainly not among the extreme. Undoubtedly this anti-immigration sentiment has in Sweden prepared the ground to a certain, though slight, extent for a positive interest in the reproduction of one's own population, once the issue has been forcibly posed and unemployment is brought down to such a low level that scarcity of openings for employment is not felt as the primary concern.

But even such international considerations and associations have certainly not been a main point. And in so far as international arguments have been raised at all, they have in any case not been of the expansionist kind but simply the fear that, if the present trend is not stemmed and reversed, the Swedish people may have a poorer chance of being left alone to mind their own business.

I am here only trying to rationalize the spontaneous reaction to the population problem in an ordinary person, a *bonus pater familias* in the meaning of Roman Law, in a small democratic country almost chemically free from imperialistic leanings. What I will maintain in the psychological question is merely that a positive attitude in this political problem is unthinkable except on the basis of the individual's identification with his nation. Without such a collective identification the attitude is quite meaningless. A pure individualism cannot even sense the goal. It should be added that without an element of collective psychology all political attitudes except irresponsible anarchism, pure and simple, are unfeasible.

In economic discussions of group interests it seems often to be forgotten that such a conception has its ground in a purely psychological assumption of an actual experience of collectivistic feelings, which in reality may be absent or present in various degrees of intensity. When, for instance, it is argued that a special group of workers in the labor market, distinguished and visible on account of sex, age, color, culture, or what not, has common interests with other workers against the employers and not with the employers against the other workers, and that the opposite idea is an illusion, the truth of the statement is entirely dependent on the subjective factor: whether there is, in fact, a sentiment of solidarity in the entire labor group or not. The term "interest" is thus subjectively determined in two dimensions: first, of course, as to individual utility, as economic analysis has always assumed, and, second, as to the degree of factual emotional solidarity ties. Particularly in the weighing of remote *contra* immediate interests is this second factor of importance.

In the present problem the thesis is that a positive response in the population problem, and its intensity, depends upon the degree of psychological identification on the part of the citizen with his nation. The relative intensity of this subjective factor should be measured, and an attempt should be made to learn what factors in the social situation determine this degree of collectivistic psychology. It is probably a function of, among other factors, social, religious, and cultural homogeneity in a national culture as it is reached through a long educational process; it should, therefore, be less marked in America than in a country like Sweden. The Swedish example shows that it does not require the stimulation of animosity toward other nations. Without doubt a nationalistic expansionism of the German type must, however, *ceteris paribus*, strengthen the feeling. To hope for a more universal collectivism than the national seems in the present stage of human history to be an illusion. No one, except in very thin intellectual strata, seems to have a working sentiment of identification with humanity or even western culture.

The attitudes toward the problem of population have a great number of other determinants than this general one which should also be studied. Without doubt the associations between the volitional element in population attitudes and in attitudes toward the whole complex of *domestic economic and social policy* are of such importance that they are next in turn to be considered.

These last-mentioned associations ought to

be considered in great detail, population attitudes being related to one after another of other political attitudes. In this very general description I am distinguishing between only two types of general political attitudes: radical and conservative. Both the political radical and the political conservative fell into a curious ideological dilemma, once the population problem in its modern import was brought to the forefront. In characterizing these dilemmas I am compelled to anticipate some of the main conclusions of later chapters, for it is obvious that the political value associations of the population problem must depend on the actual type of population policy presented for discussion with reference not only to goals but also to means.

The dilemma of the radically inclined citizen is clear. During the course of two generations political radicalism had assimilated Neo-Malthusianism and had incorporated its arguments against increase of population into its own philosophy. The stimulus to population policy which gave rise to the population crisis in Sweden did not, however, direct itself against birth control. On the contrary, it demanded the acceptance of birth control as the prime condition for a population policy which could be effective under modern conditions. The principle of voluntary parenthood was laid down as the basis for our new population policy, and it was made clear that it was neither possible nor desirable to keep up the birth rate by holding poor people in ignorance about birth control; instead, the economic, social, and psychological hindrances to child-bearing ought to be removed throughout society. An increase in population, it was furthermore made clear, was far beyond the bounds of possibility: even the more modest aim of hindering the population from rapidly vanishing was marked out as a most distant goal. To prevent a cumulatively progressive decrease in population very far-reaching social reforms would be needed.

The point now is that these reforms, the "means of the population policy," are largely of the very type which the radical-minded citizen is *for other reasons* bent on advancing. The circumstance that the population policy is thus an argument for measures for which the radical-minded citizen *desires* to find arguments is naturally of the very greatest importance in that association between attitudes in different realms which is the mechanism of the formation of political opinions. It also happens that political radicalism — albeit with a somewhat vacillating bearing and uncertain vision — identifies itself easily enough with a positive population interest. Typically, this applies in a much greater degree to young persons than to old persons, with their more rigid habits of thought; and similarly more to women, with their greater immediate interests precisely in family-social policy, than to men.

The ideological dilemma of the conservatively inclined was deeper and existed before the great crisis in opinion came. In conservatism there is, as we all know, an inclination to knit strong social values to the family and children and to the survival of the nation. These ideas have traditionally been dressed in moral norms and tied to positive adherence to religion and church, which also is part of conservative ideological patterns. In conservative circles opposition on grounds of principle to birth control had been insistently maintained. Legislation penalizing the offer for sale of and propaganda for contraceptives was enacted in Sweden in 1910 and was retained right up to 1938.

This outwardly asserted opinion of the immorality of birth control did not, however, agree any too well with individual behavior. For it could be proved in a scientifically satisfactory way that practically all non-sterile marriages — those of conservatives included — in fact practiced some form of birth control. This, by the way, also applies largely to the clergy. More particularly it could be shown that marriages in the higher economic and social strata, where political conservatism has its stronghold, utilized birth control first and most effectively, and that, in so far as ethical denouncements and state legislation hampered the spread of birth control, it was principally in the lower classes and specifically in the very poorest population groups.

To this inner moral conflict between publicly proclaimed views and private practice, which already exists, the crisis in the population problem brings a new and even more serious dilemma: the conservative-minded person has for a long time been positively inclined to the population goal as such, but now finds to his dismay that the means which are being discussed, and in part gradually applied as part of the population policy, are reforms of social policy which in political life he combats. As positive associations with the means of population policy indirectly created for the radical-minded a positive value for the aims of population policy, so in a corresponding but contrary way negative associations with these same means create for the conservative citizen a palpable indisposition toward the entire positive population alignment for which he otherwise, *prima vista*, has every sympathy.

Now it is my opinion that the ideological dilemma of conservatism in the present phase of population policy *is* past remedy — in exactly the same way as the dilemma of radical Utopianism in the population problem at the time of Malthus *was* past helping: Malthus "was right." For a time, and in extremity, conservatism rescues itself by asserting that "the population problem is in the main a 'moral' question and not an economic question" — an assertion which time and time again appears in the Swedish population debate without any proper explanation of the antithesis involved in it and without any practical proposals as to corresponding means of population policy. More and more flagrantly the "ethical" theory of population shows itself as merely an excuse for unwillingness to stand by social reform activity.

By stating these volitional associations between, on the one hand, a positive inclination to population policy and, on the other, the two extreme political ideological complexes — radicalism and conservatism — we nevertheless still move upon a very abstract and, therefore, from a sociological point of view, superficial intellectual plane. Radicalism and conservatism, especially at present, are fluid over-conceptions with quite shifting implications; in any time and place, indeed, these philosophies themselves receive their attributes and their more definite alignment from the interests and the traditions of environment of which they are merely intellectual reflections. A deep and empirical investigation would naturally have to break down this first grouping and to correlate attitudes to the population problem with much more detailed and exactly differentiated components of political ideology, and would thereby also have to work upon a classification and grouping of the ideological subjects themselves according to profession, social status, income class, and other relevant individual characteristics of importance for general political alignment.

In conducting such a study in the dynamics of political opinions and attitudes it should, furthermore, not be forgotten that the relation is not unidirectional, that it is not only *from* previous political attitudes in all other political questions *to* the population attitudes. The forming of the latter attitudes also determines attitudinal political alignments in other spheres. In a general way, it can be ascertained that the actualization of the population problem turns political opinions away from conservatism and toward radicalism. This is true as far as issues of economic, distributional, and social policy are considered. The population problem is utilized, as the conservative Swedish economist bitterly complains, as a "crowbar for social reforms."

The conservative citizen, with his honest and deep-rooted interest in family and nation, must, indeed, often find it even disgusting that this problem, which is of vital concern to him and which traditionally has furnished sublimity and elevation to his conservative political strivings, should now suddenly turn into a most dangerous weapon in the hands of his adversaries, gaining support for a remolding of society in a direction contrary to all conservative principles. So deep-rooted, however, is the moral dilemma of the true conservative that because of the population argument he will find himself, time after time, supporting items of social policy which have previously entered his mind only as dangerous radical fallacies to be combatted. It even happens that former conservatives, preponderantly intellectuals and experts such as preachers, teachers, doctors, etc., because of their interest in certain aspects of the practical population problem, turn to thoroughgoing radicalism in social policy more generally. The aggregate result, in any case, is that, although as usual in a democracy all the actual reform questions are hotly debated, the very frontier of political discussion and action has moved several miles towards the left.

If the choice of conservatism is either to be

paralyzed by inner moral conflicts or to adopt a considerable amount of radical philosophy in matters of social policy, and the end result, in both cases, involves a decrease of conservative influence on politics, the change of radicalism under the influence of the population problem is not less important. In a country where radicalism is reaching political power and control particularly, a process is for other reasons already going on through which political radicalism is gradually throwing off those elements of irresponsibility and negativism which had marked it as a secluded minority religion when it was for the most part the social protest of intellectual individuals scattered around in a society over which they had practically no real influence. This change is partly due to the power situation itself: a sense of responsibility comes with command. It is partly due to the popular support which is a prerequisite to power. The masses of a people in the various social strata, which in a democracy must be recruited under the radical banners in order to give radicalism power, understand, and respond to, positive appeals and have fundamentally strong leanings toward conservatism and scepticism; they are in this respect very different from the enlightened, basically individualistic, and often negativistic circles of the universities and liberal periodicals, and generally of the upper-class conglomerations in big cities, where radicalism is given a refuge before it acquires political status.

Well, now, on the one hand, the modern population problem strongly enforces the trend in this process. Its main political appeal is to responsibility for the survival of the nation. When this argument is incorporated in the radical philosophy it is made much easier for a large number of people to accept political radicalism. Radicalism cannot thereafter very well be depicted as a destructive force working in denial of national and family values. On the other hand, the population problem also actually strengthens the radicalism in radicalism by calling for a speeding up of the social and economic transformation of society in certain directions. These directions, as will later be developed, mean fundamentally a growth of symptomatic curative social and economic measures into prophylactic and preventive ones, a transfer of interest from social aid to social investment, and an emphasis on family before social class. This is not only another shade of radicalism; so far as actual policy goes, it is a more radical shade. But it also brings an explicit acceptance of some social values dear to the conservative-minded.

After these reflections it should not be surprising to find that the immediate actual effect of the ideological crisis in population is the creation of a political atmosphere in which vastly more radical reforms under a much wider political support can be enacted.

In the beginning I said that I intended to discuss the relation between population attitudes and other political attitudes only in the very abstract manner made necessary by not breaking down these latter attitudes into more than the two broad types of conservatism and radicalism, but I will make one exception in touching upon the interrelation between the population problem and the complex of problems concerning women's rights and their place in the social structure. This interrelation is important in itself, and the study of it will illuminate certain of the statements above.

It must here again be recalled that prior to the crisis of opinion interest in population and family was in a vague and general way kept as a conservative reserve, from which actual conservative politics could time after time be actuated with moral respectability and idealistic dignity. In the long series of combats waged over women's rights since the first half of the last century the principal argument against the emancipation measures was always anxiety for the preservation of the family. When, as in Sweden, formal equality and a liberalized marriage legislation had finally been won and the women's movement more and more zealously directed its fight against institutional barriers in the labor market in order to secure equal working opportunities and equal pay, it continually met the old conservative argument that the institution of the family, and particularly child-bearing, was in danger if women should swarm into the labor market. Woman's place, particularly the married woman's place, was in the home. Her duty was to be wife and mother; the man should, freed from her competition, be the breadwinner.

The political process was, of course, much

more complicated, but in a general way it may be stated that the fight for rights and opportunities in the wider society for married and unmarried women had as its adversaries the conservatives and the population and family arguments, while the radicals were its supporters. It is natural that in this ideological constellation radicals, and particularly progressive women, should have developed a certain animosity against the very idea of a population policy which they conceived of as a reactionary way of thinking. It must be remembered that most of the ideological influences from abroad must have strengthened that animosity. In France, the only democratic country where the population problem has played any more consistent role, a population policy was strongly supported in Catholic and conservative circles; and the new interest in population in fascist Italy and in the German Nazi movement has shown the old ideological tendency to fix woman in her place in the home.

As has already been pointed out, the population problem in its modern factual setting nevertheless has important radical possibilities. When, consequently, the problem in Sweden was taken up from the left, it also became related in a new manner to the woman question. It was pointed out that it was a natural and desirable element in social and economic development that not only men but also women should follow work from the old paternalistic family to the labor market. The possibility of women's working and earning wages was shown very often to be a condition for marriage. It was conceived to be a problem how to allow the married woman both to work and have a career and at the same time to have children. That problem, however, could not be solved by driving women back from the labor market, but only by a large number of social reforms, adjusting housing, supervision of children, and working conditions, et cetera, in such a way as to allow women to have both work and a family.[1]

Thus the opening-up of the new population discussion had two important effects. First, it allowed radicals, and particularly progressive women, to take a whole-hearted interest for the first time in population and family. The

[1] Concerning this question see Alva Myrdal's forthcoming book.

very fact, already referred to, that the new population policy turned out to imply a great number of family social reforms worked in the same direction and was, for natural reasons, particularly instrumental in leading progressive women to favor a positive population policy.

Second, it almost killed the old vague conservative idea of keeping women in the home in order to preserve the family and the nation, so strong was the force of the population argument now harnessed in front of the emancipation movement instead of in front of the conservative efforts to block women's way out of the home. For when the population problem was seriously raised and the existing tendency toward change in the family was thoroughly analyzed in its dependence on modern economic development, it turned out to crystallize itself in an irresistible argument *for* women's right to work. The success was so complete in the very first encounter that the conservative party in its own population motion in Parliament early in the year 1935 was heard to declare that now it was no longer proper to try to raise barriers against married women in work but rather to protect their right to work. This move was in flagrant contrast to the same party's attitude only the year before, when it actually had taken steps with just the contrary intention.

The very first report of the Population Commission also contained proposals to safeguard married women and unmarried mothers in public employment against being dismissed, and to increase for all women, in public service, both married and unmarried, the part of the salary retained when they were about to leave for childbirth. The proposals passed through Parliament in 1936 without meeting any serious protests. A later proposal by the Commission penalizing private employers who dismissed women employees because of marriage or childbirth, and thus guaranteeing a very important right to work for the much larger groups of women in the private labor market, has now, moreover, also been enacted by Parliament.

In the political field which concerns women's rights in the labor market the very appearance of the population problem in its modern form has thus nearly annihilated, or at least paralyzed, a whole important set of conservative ideas. It has engineered an entirely new constellation of attitudinal associations, where progressive women and, more generally, radicals are no longer compelled to fight the old conservative family values but can stand up in their own right as the spokesmen for measures to preserve the institution of the family and the nation. And the old emancipation frontier has changed into a demand for a society where women as citizens have not only equal opportunities in the labor market but at the same time the possibility of being wives and mothers. All this is only one illustration of the general statement that population policy in Sweden has now been incorporated in a liberal instead of a reactionary system of political thinking, and that it then has given a more positive content to liberal ideals and, at the same time, considerably strengthened their influence in society.

In conducting an empirical sociological study of the associations between population attitudes and the whole complex of other political attitudes, one would further have to observe the very special nature of that question among political problems in another and much more personal respect.

As was said in the first chapter, the population problem touches the sore spot of individual sexual ethics which has always been the focal point for professional moralists. It should be borne in mind how deeply complex-conditioned the sexual problem has become in western civilization. In these complex ties, emerging out of the suppressive effects on personality of the compromise between traditionally or pragmatically determined social standards and moral values, on the one hand, and individual impulses, on the other, lies, of course, the explanation of some of the startling riddles which meet the investigator when he tries to orient himself in the field of popular attitudes in the population problem.

There lies at the outset, in this psychological fixation of the population question on the individual morals of sexual conduct, a reason why the population problem can so long be kept under the threshold of popular interest, for it is of a somewhat discomforting character, one associated with a field of personal life which for the average person is deflated by a sense of guilt. Therein lies also the explanation as to why the population problem, when it finally breaks through these inhibitions and ripens into an ideological crisis in a nation, can so violently inflame public discussion, can bring about reactions of feeling that are so personal and vehement. In no other political question being debated is there such a patent psychological ambivalence at the bottom of the political reactions of in other respects nicely adjusted intellects.

Therein, finally, lies also part of the explanation as to why *the status of the individual from the family point of view* is of such extraordinary importance to his political attitude in the population problem. The old bachelor, the old spinster, the old married man, the married woman, newly married young persons, young unmarried men and women, all tend to react typically in very different ways. First and foremost, however, a strong tendency to dissimilarity in the political attitude to the population problem appears to be induced by one's possession or non-possession of children, and by how many children one has. People with many children easily arrive at a fairly complex-free, a rather humanly proud, positive attitude toward the population problem. Those without children — whether on account of sterility or strictly practiced birth control — if they are not young enough to feel like would-be parents very often have a considerably more unbalanced and complex-ridden attitude. In certain cases — on the assumption of involuntary sterility — this attitude can, instead, turn into an exceptionally strong interest in family and population policy. For the most part, however, a badly concealed resentment against the very problem makes its appearance.

Here we must recollect, furthermore, that if persons with no, or but few, children can thus for purely personal reasons be expected to display a certain feeling of resentment toward mere interest in population matters, this reaction is, naturally, strengthened by their obvious economic interests. It lies in the nature of things, as will be more closely argued in a later chapter, that the population policy in all economic classes must be based upon distributional reforms favoring families with children at the expense of bachelors of both sexes and families without or with but few children.

My hypothesis, for which I have a large, even if unorganized, experimental basis, is thus that there is a rather strong positive correlation between population attitudes and number of children. On the other hand, my experiences make me believe that persons who themselves have grown up in over-large families, particularly if economic conditions have been tight, are on the whole not only bent on practicing a very strict birth control (a considerable part of the extreme birth control in the transitional generation when it first reaches down to the lower economic strata is in all probability motivated in this biased way) but are also inclined to take a rather emotional negative attitude toward population policy. The opposite seems to be true of persons who have been only children.

It is, further, my experience that young people of both sexes, married and unmarried, acquire a positive population attitude with greater ease than older people, particularly when the latter, or their marriages, have passed out of the procreative period and thus cannot make good. In the press material there are definitely different tones in the clippings from the periodicals and papers of the youth movements (e.g., the great Social Democratic youth movement), on the one hand, and the sometimes very acid comments of the older journalists, on the other. Very definitely women generally, rather independent of age and civil status, are more positive than men, which is natural, since they actually are more concerned with family matters and suffer more from prevalent conditions, and since the proposed and hotly discussed policy was focused on marriage, family, and children. The difference in attitude between women and men is also very obvious from the clipping material.

How strongly attitudes in such problems are determined by the personal situation may be illustrated also from the adjacent field of the woman question. My observations seem to confirm, for instance, that the middle-class husband of the non-intellectual housewife very often has a strong emotional bias against the demands of other married women for the right to work. It might be argued that this is not a defense mechanism which he has built up to exalt his wife, such as she is, but that he has simply selected a wife after his own inclinations. The same middle-class man, however, when he is old enough to have grown-up daughters who try to get a living as teachers or nurses, will in all probability change his opinion. He then often turns out to have very advanced ideas as a result of the education his daughters have given him; he is then, of course, no longer defending his home-wife but his professional daughters.

All this is, as has been pointed out, only a suggestion of the hypotheses to be tested out by further research. This much seems to be established beyond doubt: that political attitudes in a problem with such intense psychological associations with the citizen's private life will to a large extent be related to, and determined by, his personal family situation. While political attitudes toward other questions are closely connected with occupation and economic and social status (i.e., with the social-group-forming characteristics of individuals), the political population problem tends, on account of its psychological association with these more personal individual characteristics, which do not constitute and are not related to social classes, to give rise to differentiations of attitudes that cut across social classes and, therefore, across political views and party alignments.

Through these personally determined associations — rooted partly in the complex-ridden sexual life of the ordinary citizen and partly in his egoistic economic interests — running counter to all social class groupings, the population problem has a certain tendency to introduce division and complication into the structure of politics. This structure is otherwise clearly demarcated according to social, occupational, and income groupings. The correlation between the structure of political parties and social classes is, naturally, weaker in a country like the United States than in a stabilized democracy like Sweden, where the party system has adjusted itself more closely to real distinctions of conflicting social ideals and group interests. Even within a less articulate two-party system of the American type, social class, and the political attitudes related to class, are of primary importance, both for party alignments and for the process by which the actual policy of one party as it appears at a certain time and place is determined.

When certain personal determinants for attitudes that have to do specifically with population are emphasized here as disturbing the determinants related mainly to class, it is admittedly only a question of tendencies among other tendencies. As a political being, a person in a modern democratic society is not only an individual, evaluating things from his own personal corner, but at the same time a member of social groups having certain broad common aims in domestic policy, and, in the last instance, a citizen of a nation with the destiny of which he identifies to a certain degree his own alignment.

Furthermore, political attitudes are not simply the mechanical outcome of these psychological forces but are always more or less under the control of rational thinking in terms of means and ends. That type of thinking, though often not very much more than a rationalization of personal prejudices, has nevertheless a tendency to suppress the purely personal discrimination of opinions; these last mentioned factors, therefore, have less force in a politically educated democracy and in those groups in such a democracy which have their ideas best controlled by systematic social and political thinking. In this whole process of the molding of attitudes and opinions a certain group-structuralization of the resultant political attitudes is accomplished little by little, with the individualization tendencies to a certain degree overcome.

But one can well understand why professional politicians must feel somewhat reluctant to raise questions which, like this, are apt to split up ideological groupings. How much simpler psychologically, then, is the problem of looking after the aged. All people count upon becoming old themselves and can easily identify themselves with the aged. Not all people, however, expect to have many children: not all of them are in a situation to do so, should they wish to.

So far it has been a question of the influence exerted *on* political attitudes in the population problem by the personal circumstances of individuals, particularly those of civil status, and of having or not having children, and of being able or not able to have children. To the sociological problem of the actual attitudes in the ideological crises, a further question of the greatest importance now attaches, a question which is, however, almost impenetrable without specially organized empirical studies. This question concerns the extent to which the political attitudes of citizens toward the population problem exercise an influence upon their individual behavior in regard to establishing families and bearing children.

The fact that it has been possible to show that practically all non-sterile families exercise some form of birth control, independently of the outwardly proclaimed view on birth control they support, comes near to indicating the non-existence of a correlation between outwardly expressed ideals and opinions — i.e., political attitudes made explicit in voting and speech-reactions, on the one hand, and personal behavior, on the other. There are, or, rather, there were before 1935 large groups and whole political parties which on grounds of principle stood against birth control. And it happens that the very social classes in which those political parties had their stronghold showed themselves to practice birth control most effectively.

If there actually were a strong direct influence from political to private attitudes, one would assume, furthermore, that the ideological crisis in the population problem during recent years in Sweden should have implied a decreased incitement to birth control and have increased child-bearing. As I stated in a foregoing chapter, however, the latest birth figures seem to imply a still declining trend: the minor rise in birth figures which revealed itself after 1934 can, in other words, be completely explained by changes in the age structure of the population and in the marriage rate, and by improving economic conditions. A positive attitude toward the nation's population problem does not seem to lead to decreased birth control in individual families. The relations between political attitudes and private behavior would thus appear to be utterly weak.

Certain signs can nevertheless be discerned that the political ideological crisis in the population problem has made children and child-bearing more popular. Women in Sweden are now much less afraid to go out and about during pregnancy than formerly. People boast more about their children. Pictures of children are being used more and more in advertising. The latest political elections in Sweden, for example, have been fought to a very great extent through an advertising apparatus which utilizes home, mother, and child as technical instruments for conveying political suggestions. Newspapers and magazines, the radio, and study activities devote more and more space to children, and so on. The beautiful young mother with healthy, lively children was for a time used as the conventional sign and symbol for everything to be stamped as progressive in the nation, from toothpaste to life insurance.

I do not wish to deny that the more positive political attitudes in the population problem through these and other indirect channels may in some degree gradually change patterns of fashion and, in time, individual behavior. And I would prefer to leave open the question whether such an influence on the part of the ideological crisis is already present. The implication would be that the birth figures in Sweden at the present time would have been at a still lower level if the crisis of opinion had not been induced.

Such a belief wins a certain support through the consideration that the ideological crisis, as it was impressed upon Swedish society, not only emphasized the desirability of reversing the fall in fertility and posed a vigorous family social policy as the chief means of accomplishing that goal but also, quite as emphatically, defended rational birth control as a natural and moral practice in all marriages, and also brought about certain public measures which had the effect of spreading knowledge of effective means of contraception more widely. The very open and intensive discussion of birth control and the incessant pointing out of the fact that children lower the level of living, and particularly that a normal number of children in the broad masses means utter poverty, must already, in the dynamic situation described, have had the effect of powerful propaganda in that direction. One of the true primary effects of the crisis must, in fact, have been increased birth control, and, particularly, there must have been more effective birth control in many social groups which earlier were backward in this respect. If, therefore, the positive suggestion of the desirability of increased fertility had had no effect at all upon people's behavior, the birth rate would probably have fallen, in spite of the rise in marriage rate because of the abnormal age distribution and the tendency of both marriages and births to rise because of improved business conditions.

I do not need to stress again how uncertain the hypotheses developed in this chapter are. They are not based merely on armchair speculation, however, but on practical experience and on a rather wide, though unsystematized, observation. They are intended as a challenge to students working on that immensely important borderland between psychology and political science which is denoted as opinion and attitude psychology. It is my feeling that methodological and experimental case work in this field of social study has come to such a point that the research itself would fare well, and certainly be of much more practical importance for both politics and social science generally, if it more commonly selected its problems and posed them out of the actual needs of social and political life.

Let me close this chapter by emphasizing again the paramount significance of our being able to specify and quantify knowledge of people's opinions and the factors which mold them. In a democracy a population policy is a *contradictio in adjecto* if, when a true understanding of the population trend is disseminated in a nation, the broad masses of that people do not react to the trend in a positive way. If, further, as I believe, the most important means of such a population policy are vast distributional reforms, these reforms must be accepted by the masses. The question is: Under what conditions and to what extent will such a popular reaction emerge out of the knowledge of the population trend?

The task before those attempting to call for such a popular reaction is, from the outset, tremendously difficult. It is not, like much other reform policy, the relatively simple question of inducing a majority to tax a minority for its own benefit. It is just the contrary: to ask a majority to tax itself severely in favor of a minority. For the majority of every population, and the great majority of a population where birth control has gone as far as it has in some western democracies, consists of citizens who are either unmarried or have no child burdens at all, or only very light ones. In Sweden, of all persons over twenty years of age not much more than a half are actually married; of those who are married only one-third actually have two or more children at home less than sixteen years of age. In spite of the fact that around 50 per cent of all children in the Swedish population are being born in families with three children and more, families with three or more children under sixteen years of age to support do not represent more than 15 per cent of all existing marriages.

For the overwhelming majority of every people, distributional reforms in the interest of the reproducing families mean economic sacrifice: for certain citizens direct diminution of personal income through increased taxation; for others, the surrender of certain measures of social policy, operating to their advantage, which could have been financed through the public budgets if the money had not been reserved for the family reforms.

When in totalitarian countries it is maintained that democratic nations will never wake up to the population problem, or, in any case, not have the popular basis for taking the necessary measures, considerations like those just referred to tend to make the statements understandable and even likely. The question remains, however, whether the citizen's psychological identification with the nation is not strong enough even in a democracy to form a basis for a positive population policy. Associations with other political attitudes complicate the picture; they do not, however, *prima facie* support pessimistic conclusions. Concerning the majority who have no immediate interest in economic population measures, further, it must be remembered that the greater part of this majority, especially during the very transitional stage when the population problem is growing acute, belongs to the younger generation; this means that, if their social valuations were such, they could feel as would-be parents, and thus also feel an indirect interest in those measures.

Perhaps it is, therefore, too early to accept the pessimistic prophecy of the opponents of democracy that it will show effeteness in facing the problem. The Swedish laboratory case study of the dynamics of popular opinion in population does not definitely point toward defeatism.

VI

EFFECTS OF POPULATION DECLINE

IN PUBLIC discussion political attitudes are naturally not given vent to as the mere articulation of wishes but are presented as rational conclusions from reasons of public welfare.

In this chapter I am thus shifting ground. From now on I shall not study the psychological problem of the manner in which people's attitudes are actually formed. I am concerned, instead, with the theoretical problem of rational aims with respect to population development, i.e., aims which can be inferred by reasoning — after a scientific analysis of the probable effects of a population decline in comparison with a stationary population trend — to be rational according to the valuations and interests current in a democratic country.

By way of introduction I will emphasize the two connections which link together the different approaches of this and the foregoing chapter. On the one hand, it is not least through a rational analysis of alternative goals that science can lead politics to greater reasoned clarity as to both objectives and means. The higher the standard of public education in a country — and the more the identification of the common citizen with his nation calls forth a widely dispersed sense of collective responsibility — the more decisive does scientifically rational guidance become for the political attitudes of the citizens and for the actual political course of events. On the other hand, the personal attitudes of the individual student, and through them the entire mental environment in which he has grown up and where he has his social moorings, *nolens volens* always color his scientific analysis to a certain degree. This last influence, which proceeds *from* the attitudes *to* the argument, is, of course, irrational in principle. One is the better protected against this source of error if one is aware of it. For this reason the sociological discussion of the last chapter is not merely important in itself but is also necessary as a preparatory cleaning of the investigator's own workshop.

The main problem in an assessment of the effects of the population development naturally concerns the economic effects.

The effect on an individual family of its abstaining from having a child, or another child, is typically to allow a somewhat higher level of living for the rest of the family. The cumulation of such decisions in the national group of many families (i.e., the fall in fertility) has, however, through its effects on the wider economic process of production, distribution, and consumption in a society, certain indirect and general effects upon the level of living in all families; these indirect effects not being simply the sum total of the individual effects. The individual direct effect is immediate; the general social effect is mostly deferred two or three decades or even more. The individual effect is a motive for individual family attitudes; the social effect is a motive for political attitudes in the population problem facing a nation, held by the individual as a citizen. The first effect is a simple matter of private budget economy. The second effect must be examined through an analysis of the entire economic system.

Such an analysis meets very great difficulties. Causal relations within future, alternatively possible population trends are naturally not, and can never be, open to direct empirical observation. By necessity the method of approach must be theoretical: first, to resolve by logical methods into its simpler elements the complex problem raised; second, to pass valid judgments on the elementary problems; and, third, to coördinate these judgments into a composite judgment valid for the total processes of social change constituting the alternatives and the lines of comparison raised in the main problem.

The theoretical analysis and synthesis involved in first resolving the problem into its elements and then composing it again does not meet insurmountable difficulties; this procedure is open to logical criticism and can be improved. The basic difficulty is, of course, to pass valid judgments on the elementary problems into which the main problem is resolved. These judgments should rightly be be founded on empirical analysis of past processes, which have been in a similar way resolved into the same elements. As historical data does not allow a laboratory technique, this empirical analysis, which should establish economics as a science, is for the most part undone. As yet, elementary causal relations are mostly not unveiled by valid empirical research; at best, large regions are covered by a very partial common-sense knowledge reached by heterogeneous and uncertain historical induction.

In this situation it is very tempting to conclude that we should never reach for knowledge concerning the future. For practical reasons, however, this conclusion is excluded. The inference would be that practical action in the political field by necessity is and must be absolutely unreasoned and irrational.

In the present problem this negative attitude would mean that, since a rational population policy would require a knowledge of the effects of population trends, no such policy with any degree of rationality is feasible. Scientists have, on the contrary, always proceeded upon the assumption that the utilization of their very inconclusive knowledge of social reality and the application of clear logic must result in an understanding *more* rational than the absolutely unguided whimsicalities of mind. No true scholar, on the other hand, pretends to anything more than a very uncertain orientation with weak lamps in the darkness of the future.

When approaching the problem of the economic effects of alternative population trends these reservations in two directions should be constantly borne in mind. A number of more specific reservations are also evident at the start. The analysis can thus hardly be carried through in common form for all countries but must be differentiated according to conditions in each separate country. The results for any particular country depend, however, among other things, upon one's conception of future conditions of foreign trade and upon the degree and efficiency of public control of economic life.

In this connection I must limit myself to some very general lines of thought. A more intensive discussion of the problem is contained in an investigation appended to the principal report of the Swedish Population Commission on the sexual question; here I can only present a very condensed synopsis of that investigation. The tentative conclusion will be that for western civilization it is probable that a higher average level of living may be attained with a stationary, rather than with a declining, population; a progressive population is, as I have tried to show, entirely out of the question and in the western world has, therefore, only a historical and academic interest.

In anticipation of this discussion, there is one thought I should like to emphasize. The effects of population on economics are not determined chiefly by the total number of the population nor by its age distribution; they are for the most part engineered by the changes in these factors. It is the *rate of change in a population during a dynamic process in time and not the quantities at any particular point of time* which are of importance in the problem.

It is on this point that theorizing has gone wrong during the last two generations, in which it has been dominated by the thought-ways most clearly expressed in the optimum population theory. As empirical statistical analysis naturally is conditioned by the theoretical questions asked — even when these questions, according to the post-war fashion of being factual and nontheoretical, are only implicit and not clearly expressed — the same criticism is valid even against attempts to study the economic effects statistically.

In the main, the same kind of reorganization of research is needed in this field as that which is being accomplished by making dynamic the research on capital formation, investment, and saving. And it is not at all astonishing that the dynamics of population should have been frequently touched upon in an entirely new way precisely in the discussion during recent years of investment and saving and of economic expansion and stagnation.

The older discussion of the economic aspects of the population problem from Malthus' time was quite simply a discussion of "overpopulation." Malthus and the generation of economists that followed after him started out from the thesis that because of the inevitable tension between procreation, which followed a geometric progression, and the means of subsistence, which at its best followed an arithmetic progression, there was maintained in the long run — aside from short-term intermediary periods when the means of subsistence jumped ahead because of improved technique or an exceptionally high mortality rate — a population so large that it could barely live and reproduce itself. That the standard of living at every point of time and under practically all circumstances should take a higher position with a smaller population was, for Malthusianism, a fundamental axiom — an axiom which was even the foundation for the theory of rent and the gradually developed general law of diminishing returns through which was determined the entire classical theory of distribution.

When afterwards, during the latter part of the nineteenth century, the pessimistic and conservative political conclusions from the theory of population were broken down because rational birth control was accepted as a theoretically possible, and morally approved, method for hindering the press of the population against the means of subsistence, population theory, nevertheless, continually took form according to the supposition that the real problem was and always would be the menace of overpopulation. This position dominated economic discussion until the Great War and even thereafter. Few economists with professional self-respect — and, as far as I know, none in the Anglo-Saxon and Scandinavian neoclassical line — had any other thought than that, even if an active pressure against the means of existence was not present in the old meaning, nevertheless the lower the population, the higher the average level of living would ordinarily be. The classical inheritance of thought completely dominated economic thinking in this respect. The rapid expansion of the population throughout the whole century strengthened the tendency to fear overpopulation as the outcome of the population trend.

Neoclassical economic theory was particularly fettered by its static approach to its problems. The static principle was, in fact, much more fundamentally embodied in the theoretical structure of neoclassical marginalists than in earlier classical theory. It has important associations with the liberalist noninterference bias of the whole school. It is not difficult to ascertain that this school of economists on the whole even showed a tendency to minimize actual changes as far as the future was concerned. Thus the idea was always maintained that the tempo of technical progress in the future could be expected to become slower.

A very amusing set of quotations could be collected from economic literature showing how, decade after decade, and particularly, of course, in depressions, it was predicted that no further technical progress of large economic importance would be accomplished. The authors always had the great inventions behind them and only "minor improvements" ahead. This list could, as is well known, be continued by quotations from very representative authors until the present time. The psychology behind these systematically iterated mistakes is very simple indeed. It takes quite a capacity of imagination to foresee the branching out of new inventions from recent discoveries and the implications of their practical application, but, as one looks back, this branching out, which makes a discovery epochal, is a matter of common historical knowledge.

This idea of the decreasing tempo of technical development from the present point onward was a comfort greatly needed by static economic theory. It also agreed well with the quite exaggerated respect for the extraordinary efficiency of private capitalistic enterprise which was nursed by the liberalist tradition of economics. It was, particularly in the generations preceding the war, not considered exactly tactful to imagine that very extensive improvement of production was still possible. In America, however, where until the recent long stagnation industrial development followed a still hotter pace, it was impossible to maintain this static pessimistic view of future technical development. Instead, the hypothesis was there worked out that technical development was proportional to the amount of technical knowledge accumulated at any point of time and, consequently, that it would rise progressively according to the continuous interest formula. *Prima facie*, this hypothesis seems more realistic. The present American economic stagnation and the economic difficulties in several other countries can, I am inclined to believe, be fully explained without resorting to a deceleration of technical progress.

Per se, technical progress represents increased power over the forces of nature — increased "natural resources," as one could rightly say, looking on the matter from the economic point of view. Economic theory stressed, instead, *scarcity* of natural resources. Now this point of view is not precisely the one which is forced upon us by closer study of economic facts today. The western world does not seem to suffer from any lack of natural resources. The fault is rather with the demand. Or, to put it more correctly and completely, what we lack is a rational and planned social organization of production and distribution. We have plenty of the means of production, as well as technical knowledge of how these should be used in order to maintain and raise our level of living, but we do not master the organization of production and distribution. Society is still our least efficient machine.

It actually took us an unnecessarily long time before we discovered that the main trouble was not any lack of natural resources, so fixedly have we held to the static thoughtways of the liberal economists — the apologetics of the world as it is and the opponents of public interference. Even in the post-war period this make-believe scarcity of natural resources has hypnotized the minds of politicians in the very face of continually falling prices of raw materials, a mistake which, by the way, is probably not guiltless in the most disturbing political development. And the crises that have occurred of superabundance and market disorganization — "plenty of wheat and no bread" — have been repeatedly asserted to be paradoxical, which they most certainly are from the static viewpoint of scarcity economics.

As long as the main cause — and justification — for common poverty could be assumed to be scarcity, scarcity of natural resources and capital, it was natural to believe that a decline of population would decrease this scarcity and raise standards of living. When, as now, interest is focused instead upon the institutional machinery of production and consumption, this conclusion is not so obvious. A shrinkage of population would not in itself make this machinery run more smoothly. As we shall find, there are reasons for an opposite opinion.

The existence of unemployment is one of the extremely disturbing effects of the lack of social organization in production and distribution. The inference that the population is "too large," at least by the amount of the unemployed is, however, invalid. If we could "wish away" from the country and the world all the present unemployed, this change would bring about secondary changes in the various supply and demand curves, with the result that in the lapse of a short time a new unemployment would develop, although perhaps not so large as before the change. The important thing is, however, that the population factor which is assumed to be changeable is not the death rate among unemployed, but fertility. A lowered birth rate would not affect the present number of unemployed at all; its possible effect is deferred fifteen or twenty years. And there is no *a priori* reason why, after the course of such a period of time, a lower rate of unemployment should be expected as a result of lowered fertility, if this particular change is not assumed to improve the social organization of the economic process.

Let us go back to the scarcity theory of the liberal school of economists. The static approach was early crystallized in the theory of an optimum population. This theory is in reality very old. From the standpoint of the history of doctrine there is a certain interesting shade of difference between the classical and the neoclassical variation of this theory which I shall pass over. In its neoclassical form it has been most clearly set forth by Wicksell. With much the same substance, it has been appropriated by most economists and statisticians who have dealt with the population question.

The theory of an optimum population does not belong to the more complicated economic theories. It is, quite simply, as follows: that the highest possible average level of living (greatest national income *per capita*) is attained with a certain size of population, a size which was usually assumed to be considerably smaller than that existing. With any change from this optimum position, whether the movement be upward or downward, there is brought about a lower average level of living. This curve, which reaches its maximum in the optimum population and which denotes the dependence of the average level of living on the size of the population, is, according to the theory, dominated by two counteracting forces. The first force is quite simply the law of diminishing returns: since, *ceteris paribus*, with a smaller population the total amount of land and durable real capital is greater per inhabitant, the marginal productivity of labor and even the average amount of production per worker becomes greater the smaller the population, and *vice versa*. The opposite force is the law of external economics: there are certain advantages dependent on division of labor with a larger population by reason of which the law of diminishing returns cannot prevail down to the smallest population size imaginable. At the position of optimum population the two forces evenly counterbalance one another, resulting in a maximal welfare of the population. Above the optimum position the law of diminishing returns has most effect; under that level the law of external economics dominates.

The theory of optimum population proceeds from two common-sense observations, which have the character of *reductiones in absurdo* of the contrary opinion that population size is entirely without influence on the average level of living. These observations are that, assuming a low international division of labor, a very great density of population will necessitate an existence on the level of misery, as will, likewise, a very low density of population. If people are very numerous in relation to the means of existence — e.g., if humanity were enclosed in one of the smaller Swiss cantons — they will certainly starve to death. If, on the other hand, they are so few and scattered over so wide an area that coöperation on a social scale is precluded, they have, of course, to give up everything that requires a more highly integrated social organization. But in order to deal with the pressure of population in China or India — and, for that matter, in certain backward and culturally isolated regions in the United States or Poland — or with the indigence of life in a desert land, one does not really need such a factitiously constructed general theory. What the optimum population theorists actually had in mind was, instead, the ordinary western countries in process of rapid industrialization. They therefore interpolated a curve between the two self-evident extremes of utter poverty and formulated a social law on this curve which then was interpreted by the two laws of return already referred to.

I cannot stop to give a thorough criticism of the optimum population theory. For the present purpose it may be enough to hint at some of the points where caution is to be prescribed.

As to the curve itself obtained by this hazardous interpolation — the average level of living as a function of population density — it should be noted that there is actually nothing in its construction which indicates that it could not, for large spaces, have a very level course. It is, likewise, perfectly possible that this curve might have several maximum positions at very different sizes of population and that the difference in height of the average level of living between the maximum positions might be unimportant, particularly in view of the great indeterminateness in theoretical content which the quantity "level of living" shares with all averages and indices. In both cases the conclusion would be that average level of living should be fairly independent of population size for certain values of this last quantity.

It is further clear, and also recognized, that not only the average level of living at any population size but, more primarily, the forms of the productivity functions which are supposed to determine the curve must be thought of as depending upon the available technique. As the amount of applicable technical knowledge is changing and increasing all the time, the assumed curve, and the optimum position, cannot be projected into the future simply on static assumptions. If, then, the curve is supposed to be changing under the influence of future technical change, this makes the theory more valid *in abstracto* in this particular respect, but at the same time increases the difficulties in practical application tremendously.

I shall not go on with this theoretical criticism, even though the points raised are far from inclusive, but conclude with the remark that it has, of course, never been possible anywhere to give for any country a quantitatively expressed answer to the practical question of the actual position of this population optimum. The theory is a speculative figment of the mind without much connection with this world; it does not give any guiding rule for the practical and political judgment of reality. Actually, the theory has mostly been utilized to furnish a broad and vague foundation for the opinion that the level of living should be higher with a smaller population. The argument is simply that, after a certain point of very low population density, the law of diminishing returns must dominate.

Curiously enough, in this neoclassical speculation on population the factor of age distribution was for a long time not studied, and it was never studied intensively as to its economic implications. It is remarkable, because this factor could to a large extent be taken care of in a stationary model of theory. When a certain trend of the population development is maintained for such a long period that a *stable age distribution* has been reached, the difference between a progressive, a stationary, and a regressive population — apart from a different development of population numbers — is that in the first more than in the second, and in the second more than in the third, the number of children is relatively large and the number of old people relatively small. A corresponding difference rules even within each major age group taken by itself. If we thus compare a regressive population with a stationary one, we find that in the first young children are relatively fewer than older ones and that the center of gravity is also higher in middle age as well as in old age.

Now people in different ages are productive in different degrees, and — within a given standard of living — their consumptive demands, their cost of living, also differ. Here intensive empirical studies ought to set in, and they are now being made in Sweden, to ascertain the average productivity and the cost of living in different age groups. These calculations give somewhat different results in different social classes. The occupational and cultural changes also alter the quantities from time to time very considerably.

I cannot in this short synopsis enter upon the details of how such realistic studies of age-differential productivity and cost of living are to be planned and carried out. One very broad generalization must suffice. If, by combining productivity and cost of living into a *net productivity*, we try to get a general index for the contribution or noncontribution of various age groups, we get, of course, the general picture that normally a person during two periods of his life, the beginning and the end, consumes without producing, while during a period between he produces more than he actually consumes. The influence of its age structure on the average level of living of a nation will then be determined by the relation between the "overproducing" and the "overconsuming" age groups.

Now it happens, as everybody familiar with demographic problems knows, that rather independently of the course of population development, if the trend is stable, the sum of children and old people is in a pretty fixed relation to the whole population. In a stationary population there are more children and youngsters but fewer old people than in a regressive population. From the point of view of society as a whole it is of less importance that, under the ruling norms and valuations embodied in the prevalent type of family organization, the children are usually provided for by their parents, while the old people are supposed to be living on their own savings. In the national economy the maintenance of children and saving for one's old days should come to very much the same thing.

There is, however, one important difference. A declining population will be relatively somewhat richer than a stationary one, and a stationary one richer than a progressive population, for there will be less need of investment for keeping up or enlarging the productive and consumptive capital apparatus. *If* we could assume a perfectly balanced capital market — in this assumption is hidden the principal shortcoming of the stationary analysis — the corresponding part of excess monetary saving in a declining population could be utilized to raise the level of living somewhat. This is due, however, not to the difference in age structure, which, as has been pointed out, is of minor importance, but to the general shrinkage of population in its relation to the amount of capital equipment. This is the basic consideration in the theory of optimum population which we will have to come back to.

Age distribution as such should, in any case, have very little influence on the standard of living of a population. It must be said again, though, that this is a very broad generalization. In a more intensive study we should also have to investigate the effects of declining mortality on the stable age distribution, and we should have to split net productivity into its production and consumption sides and the major age groups into smaller age groups. We should further have to consider the big differences in different social classes and occupations as to the length of the periods in which young and old people are allowed to consume without producing and as to their relative consumption, and we should also have to observe the effects of occupational and cultural change. Our rather intensive studies after these lines in Sweden suggest, however, that the broad generalization will on the whole keep valid in spite of the great occupational changes going on as a result of industrialization, and in spite of the rising standard of living and of social and educational reforms. The trend of population development should not in itself, *via* this factor, have much influence on the economic welfare of a people.

One important reservation must, however, be added at once. Such a statement holds true only when a stable age distribution is reached. When, as now in the whole western world, the population trend changes in a short period from a progressive to a regressive type, we have an interregnum of abnormal age distribution, where the children are few in number, corresponding to a regressive population trend, but the old people also are relatively few, corresponding to the earlier progressive trend. For a few decades — and assuming that unemployment is not increased, an assumption which is part of the general assumption of static equilibrium underlying the whole theory — this must form another factor tending to raise the standard of living. This factor is transitory; it disappears as soon as the age distribution approaches its stabler form. Moreover, if the population at any time should return to full reproduction again and stop the shrinkage, a corresponding transitory press downward on the level of living would result.

At this point a stationary analysis has to stop. The fundamental weakness of the theory is, however, that it is static. It does not allow for the dynamic factors. It relates the level of living merely to *size of population* and eventually, if elaborated in this direction, to *age structure*. Like the whole type of economic speculation of which it is an outgrowth, it merely compares two different positions, without allowing for the effects of the change between them. An analysis that proceeds must attach importance to the fact that there is actually a *development in time* between the two positions compared in the stationary analysis, and must study the effects of the *change* of quantities from one position to another.

The major dynamic effects of a change from a progressive to a regressive population trend — or generally of a lowering of the population trend — must be related to the decreased rate of increase of production (and consumption). If technical progress *per se* can be assumed to be independent of the population trend, this effect is evident. It has sometimes been held that technical progress is more rapid when the population trend is higher; in any case the opposite relation has never been vindicated.

If the change in population trend should not result in any disturbance of economic stability, the decline in increase of production should not occur before the time when the lowered fertility has had its result in the numbers of persons of working age (fifteen to twenty years later). In the meantime the effect would only be certain changes in the direction of consumptive demands and, consequently, of production. These changes are very much of the same type as other changes in demand functions constantly going on in a dynamic society. They might well be important enough in their disturbing effects on production, however, to counterbalance the increase in *per capita* real income (consumption and saving) which we have shown should be the transitory result of an unstable age structure. As the age structure becomes stable these extra disturbances of demand function will disappear. As then a continuous decrease in the working ages is being effected, a general (relative) shrinkage of production and consumption will take place.

According to the stationary analysis this shrinkage should be followed by a rising level of living, in so far as the law of diminishing returns dominates. The marginal productivity of the human factors of production, and also their average earnings, should increase. One general assumption underlying this conclusion is the atomistic supposition that the total real capital in a society is fluid and fungible as the money captial is. Now, real capital — including all natural resources — is instead embodied in the production apparatus. This structure is fixed. Every change means a value-destruction of existing real capital. These losses might be large enough to counterbalance the assumed increase of capital goods *per capita*. They might even be larger — indeed, much larger.

The point can be illustrated by the capital invested in apartment houses and homes; in Sweden nearly half of the normal investment is in housing. An adjustment of this stock of consumption capital goods to a smaller number of families is not possible except under heavy capital losses. Now, it is true that the same occurs as a result of the normal rise of the housing standard under any population trend (e.g., under the earlier progressive trend). But the important reservation should be added that — assuming the same average rise in the housing standard — the higher the population trend, the smaller the proportion of housing capital which has to be scrapped or rebuilt.

It can further be maintained quite generally that every shift in the demand curves for capital goods, due to whatever primary cause of change, which in a progressive system of production and consumption will only cause a corresponding shift of new investments followed by a rapid restoration of the supply-demand balance, in a stationary and still more in a shrinking economic system will result in a prolonged disbalance. (The length of time is determined by the relative lowness of the population trend and by the durability of the capital goods in question.) For the owners of capital the disbalance means losses. The anticipation of the increased possibility of such losses increases investment risks all around. Let me illustrate the point by returning again to housing.

In a rapidly growing city a relative overproduction of a certain type of housing accommodations — say apartments of a certain size — is not a very serious affair. The construction of such buildings has only to stop for a short period, allowing the population to grow to fit the too-large capital structure, and such a reaction on the part of the investors is a natural outcome of the forces in the market. In a stationary or, still more, in a regressive city the mistake in investment, and consequently the loss, is irremediable; there are, and will be, too many of those buildings.

Very much the same thing is true not only for housing capital but for the whole structure of the apparatus of capital production. The risk of wasteful disproportions and maladjustment in capital investment, and of subsequent losses, increases when the population is not constantly growing to fit even the wasteful mistakes of individual entrepreneurs and the unforeseen changes in demand curves. The risks of entrepreneurs will, therefore, increase, and their willingness to invest decrease. It must be remembered that one of the basic conditions of the whole liberalist order of capitalistic society, where individual entrepreneurs act independently in a free and unregulated market, and, more particularly, one of the basic conditions of the possibility of assuming that their uncoördinated actions do not lead to too much waste is a rapidly growing society. The retardation of market increase has the effect of increasing risks in all capitalistic enterprise and, consequently, of hampering private investment.

Private investment is depressed by a lowered population trend in another way, too (i.e., even apart from the increased risks for *Fehlinvestierungen*). In ordinary western society, where the standard of living is continually rising, there will always be a tendency to have too much real capital which, directly or indirectly, serves the needs of a formerly more common lower level of living (e.g., small-sized apartments). When the national household is increasing rapidly, this fact does not disturb investment very much. Investment has only to be turned more to the type of real capital that directly or indirectly serves the needs of a higher standard, and this is also the effect of the forces in the market. When, however, the population is becoming stationary, and even more when it is beginning to shrink, the whole situation changes. To stick to the example above, smaller apartments will then be relatively very cheap and people will cling to that standard of housing, even if they could afford to live in larger and better apartments. The existing stock of apartments of a lower standard will then block the tendency to raise the housing standard. It should be mentioned that this example is not an imaginary one but that it gives the gist of experiences which have been studied in some detail in Sweden. In different degrees the same holds true in the whole structure of the capital apparatus of society. The result is, on the side both of consumption demand and of production demand, a drying-up of the very sources of the inducements to invest. It may be answered that the individual savings set free by the lower standard in certain items of the consumption budget can be, and ordinarily will be, utilized to raise standards and demands in other directions. Since, however, the subnormal demand is directed toward consumption that requires large investments — it is the very fact that these investments are durable and represent a proportionally very large part of certain consumption costs which under the circumstances keeps these particular costs and the corresponding consumption standard down — the compensatory demands in other directions will not create an equal demand, direct and indirect, for investment. The final outcome must, therefore, be a decreased stimulus to investment.

To be more specific I have talked here in terms of capital goods of higher and lower standards. It should be pointed out, however, that the same holds true for every shift in the demand curves. *If* productive or consumptive demand for a thing is shrinking, *in so far as* the demand is served by a product in which durable capital goods are employed to such an extent that remuneration for them is a relatively large portion of total costs, a low population trend will incline to keep these costs subnormal and retain consumption in spite of the initial change in the demand. Investment in the particular type of capital goods affected by the decreased demand will naturally cease, and as the compensating increases of demand in other directions made possible by the consumers' savings cannot be assumed to be directed to the same extent to capital goods, a tendency toward decreased inducement to invest capital must result.

Thus for two specific reasons — the increased risks in all sorts of investments and the decreased demand for capital goods serving a higher standard of living or new demands generally — we may expect a lowered population trend to have a hampering influence on the total amount of private investment in a society. On the other hand, we had previously reached the conclusion that a declining population in comparison with a stationary, and a stationary in comparison with a progressive, have on the whole a smaller need for investment to maintain and increase the productive and consumptive apparatus and, because of that, a relatively greater amount of available savings. Our two specific factors actually hampering investment will thus work in an environment where there is already an increased permanent risk of disbalance between saving and investment.

Now, modern theory of the cyclical and secular changes in the condition of business and production has come to fix more and more attention on investment as a driving force in economic progress. Savings which are not invested only raise the total of losses in society. If a lowered population trend hampers investments, it curtails progress and increases unemployment and poverty. These effects can easily assume much larger proportions in an industrial society than the results of the static forces tending to make a smaller population richer in capital resources *per capita*.

The possibility is, of course, open that government can decrease investment risks — initially increased by the lowered population trend — by central planning and investment control, the state thus assuming the coördination of the actions of individual entrepreneurs which was less essential when population was continually growing into investment mistakes and changes of demand. The state can also increase inducements to investment in the higher standard capital goods by subsidizing a higher standard of living in those directions or by directly subsidizing such investment. The state can also even compensate for the falling off of investment by its own investments, which then, from the point of view of the balance between saving and investment, may be in other fields. And, certainly, the trend in population will turn out to be one of the strongest underlying forces promoting government control and participation in business and production. But *per se* the lowered trend in population, because of these dynamic factors, will give rise to a tendency toward a more depressed state of production, hampered enterprise and employment, and, consequently, consumption standards.

It is, of course, difficult to ascertain the due weight of these dynamic factors; they will, moreover, have very different weight in different countries, and, as has already been said, their effects can be counteracted by government interference.

The aging of the population must also be considered in this connection. I will restrict myself to quoting the conclusion which the Swedish Population Commission reached on this point:

A declining population means a relatively greater number of old people and a higher average age even within the generation of middle-aged persons. Because of certain average psychical differences between generations, which have not been well studied, such a difference in age distribution must have important effects upon the whole life of the people, not only economically but even politically and culturally.

In a judgment of this question it is certainly incorrect to underestimate the importance of the calm presence of mind, the patient care, and the greater experience of life which comes with age. But the age distribution already present with a stationary population should give assurance of a sufficient predominance by the older classes which possess these valuable qualities in high degree. The age distribution which comes about with a declining population would, on the other hand, imply serious danger that the nation will be wanting in the other qualities likewise valuable, which belong above all to youth: willingness to sacrifice, courage, power of initiative and creative imagination.

For my part I should like to add parenthetically the reflection that, when I seek to understand the unprecedentedly tragic post-war history, I cannot avoid the thought that the cause in part lies in the lack of young people in the great European nations which took part in the war. It was the young generation, and the best of it, that bled to death on the battlefields, while remaining to organize peace again were the older generation, the white-feathered stay-at-homes, and a shattered, war-neurasthenic remainder of the youthful generation.

This question of the relative value of the different age groups in a society I will, however, leave aside. But in this connection I want to emphasize another point. The shifting of the age distribution *within* the working ages, which will result from the lowering of the population trend, will come to have a restrictive effect upon *young people's opportunities for advancement* in all the occupational groups where there is a career to carry out. It may, it is true, be easier for young people to "get into" a job, but it will be more difficult to "get ahead." With a declining population, as opposed to a stationary one, and along with it an average decrease of personnel in all spheres of activity, there will be a larger percentage of older persons everywhere who can hold appointments by right of seniority. It will then take a longer time for a young person to arrive at a responsible and leading position, and the probability that he ever will get there will vanish. There thus lies in the actual age structure of a declining population a tendency to restrict the opportunities of youth.

In all occupations in which careers are possible, the working personnel is organized hierarchically. Every part of the working life has the form of a pyramid with a broad base which rapidly tapers toward the top. Society consists from this point of view, quite simply, of a conglomeration of such hierarchical pyramids: if one adds them all together he gets an aggregate hierarchical pyramid which is the present social order. This aggregated hierarchical pyramid of society, where the abscissa is the number of individuals and the ordinate their occupational stratum, as also their social and income position, has, as we all know, a sharply tapering form; the tendency in social development for decades has, in fact, been that the number of superior persons steadily decreases in relation to the number of subordinate persons.

The able-bodied adult population must be pressed into this hierarchical pyramid of society. This always frustrates the human material: the larger number are never able to achieve the careers they hope for. Many personal ambitions must be cut short. But it is clear that the more progressive the population trend is, the better will the ordinary pyramid of age structure correlate with the hierarchical pyramid of employment opportunities: thus a larger proportion of the young can get ahead in life. The more regressive the population, the less there is of such a correlation. The greater the difficulties in the way of ambitious youths, the more people even in the higher ages will be held at the bottom of the hierarchical pyramid; and social rises will occur less often and with more difficulty. In a declining population the hopes of the individual must to a greater extent be disappointed, his possibilities for development be cut off. This is another way in which a lowered population trend dampens the whole spirit of society, decreases the tempo of its progress.

We have already pointed out that the expansionist capitalistic system of private enterprise had as one of its prerequisites a progressive population. A declining population will increase investment risks all around and, even apart from that, will lessen the demand for new investment. Since in an aging society monetary savings are kept up, the result will be a continuous tendency toward investment falling short of saving. The government will have to step in, controlling and coördinating individual enterprise and compensating for the shortage in investment opportunities. But it will have a difficult task, if it is not to replace private enterprise over the whole field.

In addition to this there are the hampering effects on inter-class mobility of the change in age structure. And it is difficult to avoid another broad generalization here: the mental and spiritual basis of private capitalism was the opportunity for individual advancement, the belief in which acquired an almost religious intensity in the "American dream" which stands as the creation of the country with the most steeply progressive population, the most unhampered private enterprise, and the most fervent individualism. When on account of the changed age structure individual opportunities to rise socially are blocked, people will get discouraged. They will lose their dynamic interest in working life; society will lose the mental attitude that goes with progress. Interest in security will be substituted for an earlier interest in social advancement.

The peculiar brand of Socialism which is apt to develop under the continued influences of these factors must unfortunately be expected to take on an administrative, bureaucratic, senile character; it will be the bureaucratic administration of the liquidation of a people. Much less takes care of itself in a declining economy than in one that is growing; the bureaucratic apparatus must therefore increase. This apparatus becomes less dynamic, less effective, not only because it comes to rest principally in the power of old men, but also because of a heretofore unmentioned reason: the best, the most dynamic intelligences cannot come to feel a very great interest in the administration of a liquidation. Even one who was a Socialist in politics, but who has felt the pulse of progress in his veins, who has loved free initiative and advance, must feel cheerless before these prospects. He hardly expected this to be the outlook for Socialism. He would even be tempted to defend private capitalism if by that means he could revivify dynamic progress.

In discussing the dynamic effects of the changed age structure under a lowered population trend, our point of view has been that of young people looking toward the future. The main burden, however, will fall on the older age groups. When they increase in relative numbers it will not only block advancement for young people; at the same time, and primarily, it will increase their own difficulties in keeping employment.

Of these two effects, the first will dominate relatively more in the middle-class occupations, with their more fixed rules for advancement in income and security in accordance with age and their greater adherence to the seniority principle. The latter effect will dominate the immense realm of common labor. In both fields the two effects will be simultaneously in operation. Thus, in the middle-class occupations the older generation will be large enough both to hamper the advancement of the young and to make positions uncertain for themselves. In the common labor market the structuralization of the conditions for employment and advancement, partly as a result of the efforts of trade unions, is constantly creating a situation similar to that in the middle-class occupations, regulating the right to employment and advancement in the interest of the workers already in employment, so that newcomers have to serve several years in order to reach the surer and better-paid jobs. In the face of a changing age structure these attempts will, however, meet difficulties.

When the regressive population trend has been working long enough so that the generation of youth which has just arrived at the working age begins to be fewer in number than the generation which stands next highest in age — and particularly after the development of population has reached the point where the young generation coming into employment is less than that going out of employment because of death or old age — it should, of course, be easier for these young workers to get into the labor market, even if advancement is more difficult. Opposite this tendency, however, one must place the tendency toward a generally more depressed economic situation as a result of such a population development. It is very uncertain whether the favorable tendencies of such a development will overbalance the unfavorable for the younger generation. The great importance of the actual business situation in general for the placing of the younger workers on the labor market is clearly evident from the especially large cyclical variations in the unemployment of youth. During the last boom in Sweden unemployment of youth was lowered to a minimum, in spite of the fact that the yearly number of youths arriving at the age for employment is still relatively large.

For older workers the situation in the labor market is poorer with a regressive population development both because of their becoming relatively greater in numbers and because of the generally more depressed state of business. For them the two tendencies run together. If, in the future, we should have to reckon with a continued general rise of the demand for quality of work — because of rationalization, standardization of labor conditions, etc. — the situation in the labor market might become quite difficult for workers at the ages of forty, fifty, and sixty, as their relative numbers increase in the regression of population.

The very fact that the older workers have acquired a specialized training through their earlier work experiences, and because of that are not fungible as the young workers just entering the labor market are, will turn out to be increasingly a cause of insecurity. In this respect the older workers are under a danger similar to that of the capital apparatus when the population trend is lowered. Every slacking-off of relative demand for a particular kind of worker, which in a growing economy could easily have been adjusted to by the market reaction that young workers would cease to be recruited for that field, will now fall with full force on the workers already there. This last point is the more serious from the point of view of social policy because the problem of the occupational guidance of youth, which in my country as in others has not been satisfactorily solved, is a relatively very easy problem compared with that of giving new training and greater scope of opportunity to older workers who, in the processes of economic adjustment, have been put out of employment. And it must be remembered that everything which it becomes necessary to do in such a situation in order to defend the older worker's right to work and achieve security will have a tendency to decrease the opportunity for "getting in" which the young workers have under a lowered population trend.

Apart from this growing conflict of interests between young and old workers — and, more particularly, the increased danger to old workers that, like the apparatus of capital, they will be made obsolete by every tendency toward occupational shifts — there is, in the main, no reason to differentiate a special labor market problem within the larger problem of the economic effects of the population trend which is here dealt with. It is certainly true that political, organizational, and other institutional changes can influence labor conditions away from the direction which they would take if they were determined solely by the general economic development. But such reforms do not depend upon the population development, at least not in a direct and very important manner. This means that if, as is here thought to be likely, a lowered population trend on the whole can be expected to have generally depressive effects on investment and production, it follows that labor will be placed in a poorer position.

As to agriculture, one word should be said. In the western countries a rapid industrialization has been constantly going on. In countries like Sweden and America this change is far from having reached its limits. It is a condition of a rise in standard of living that a portion of the family income that is absolutely increasing but relatively decreasing shall be set aside for food. Similarly, it is also a condition for this development that a decreasing part of the population shall be engaged in agriculture.

If, now, a lowered trend of population has a generally depressing influence upon industrial production and investment, a barrier might be built against this natural transference of labor from agriculture to industry and the whole process of continued industrialization might be hampered. As the elasticity of demand for agricultural goods is generally low, the resultant poverty in agriculture could be very intense. In agricultural regions during such a process a situation might develop in which there was an actual "overpopulation" in a very real sense, particularly as fertility has a tendency to keep up for a long time in poverty-stricken rural districts.

That such a situation is not a proof of general overpopulation in a country or in the western world as a whole is the more palpable from our previous discussion, since it might result from the lowered population trend which has contributed to the industrial stagnation, which in its turn has hampered the shift of the population from agriculture to industry.

In concluding this chapter I do not need to emphasize how weakly founded the conclusions are, and must be, for reasons pointed out in the beginning of the discussion. I have merely tried to bring out certain general relations and state hypotheses which should be tested out in more intensive research. Such research cannot be carried out in a general way but must be related to the specific situation of each country and each time.

I believe, however, that I have given a general, though vague, defense, even from the point of view of economic effects, for proceeding in the following analysis of population policy from the general premise that in a country where continued industrialization is not blocked a stationary population is preferable to a declining one (a progressive population being entirely out of reach).

VII

POPULATION POLICY

IN ORDER to rationally establish a goal for population policy the effects of alternative population trends should be investigated as intensively as possible. Not only should economic effects be studied but also effects in other realms. As different population trends mean differing sizes of families, the effects of children and of the number of children upon happiness in marriage should be studied, as also the educational situation of children in families of different sizes. All effects in these and other respects should be weighed according to the prevalent interests and ideals in democratic society, and it should be observed that these valuations may differ for different groups.

Without going further into the discussion of effects, interests, ideals, and, consequently, population goals, I shall from now on proceed upon the assumption that the goal is *a constant population in the long run*, i.e., 100 per cent net reproductivity. The Swedish Population Commission established this goal as a premise for its work. A higher trend seems unattainable. The question of whether a population increase shall be aimed at, therefore, becomes purely academic and need never be debated. The practical alternatives are a more or a less rapid decrease in population, with a stationary population as the upper limit. Our assumption means that this limit should be aimed at.

It is to be expected that this population goal must sooner or later become the aim upon which population policy in every country in the western world will be compelled to direct all its efforts. For a lower reproduction level would be accompanied by a progressively advancing shrinkage of the population. Let us suppose, for the sake of the argument, that in a given country a *certain* population decline should be accepted; there must, however, be a level below which public opinion would not like the development to continue. The practical problem, when this limit is approached, will be to raise net reproduction to 100 per cent. At one level or another in the population decline to be expected, the desideratum must come to be a population which reproduces itself.

To the assumed goal for population development corresponds, as we have already seen, a certain distribution of individual families according to size types. Thus the fulfillment of this norm for population policy is incompatible not merely with the "two-child system" advocated by Neo-Malthusianism, but also with a "three-child system." In fact, our population goal almost implies that the ordinary non-sterile marriage should aim at four children. This translation of the general population goal into a requirement for individual family behavior is based upon marriage and mortality rates of approximately the level prevailing in Sweden, which will be used again in this chapter as a convenient point of reference.

The widely held opinion of the sufficiency of a lower average fertility arises from a failure to study the division of families according to family size in a stationary population. Above all, the large number of involuntary sterile marriages is very often overlooked. It is estimated that in Sweden nearly 10 per cent of all marriages are entirely sterile, that perhaps a further 7½ per cent become sterile after the birth of one child and an additional 5 per cent after the birth of two children. This implies that more than one-fifth of all marriages are prevented from producing more than two children, of whom nearly half will be entirely childless. This estimate is very loose, naturally enough, but it nevertheless suggests the extent of sterility and semi-sterility. It has furthermore been overlooked that, in addition to these sterile marriages, a large number of marriages under all social conditions and for various reasons — late marriage, illness, or poverty, for instance — will be voluntarily childless or have but few children. The population policy must be applied to the remaining families, which then, if the population is to remain stationary, must aim at a considerably high average number of children.

My starting point is, furthermore, that such a reproduction balance will not establish itself automatically. There is nothing which suggests that a 100 per cent net reproduction represents a level of fertility at which the national aggregate of individual families will mysteriously hold themselves of their own accord. On the contrary, everything indicates that a fertility rate necessary to maintain a population equilibrium is not in prospect, under social and economic conditions now prevalent for the formation of families, and that the tendency is in the direction of a productivity rate of less than 50 per cent rather than more than 50 per cent; and this, of course, implies a very rapid depopulation.

It is fairly evident to everyone who has studied the population development in all its social and cultural aspects that the political problem of realizing a 100 per cent net reproduction, at any population level whatever, is perhaps hopeless. Even though a very pessimistic view must be taken of the problem of the possibilities of setting a halt to depopulation, efforts nevertheless must not be relinquished. Public opinion in all the countries of the western world will demand such a policy within a relatively short time. The question is, how will it appear?

At the outset it is obvious that a certain improvement in the balance of births and deaths can be accomplished merely through a reduction of mortality. For natural reasons only that diminution of mortality which concerns the age classes within the fertility range plays any permanent role in the reproduction of a people.

As all are aware, it is with regard to infant mortality that the possibilities of improvement are of greatest quantitative importance. Even in a land with such a relatively high and even standard of living and such relatively good hygienic conditions — and such a small number of children in a family — as my reference country, Sweden, about every twentieth child dies before reaching the age of one year. Intensive investigations of infant mortality in different income and social classes in the capital of the country, Stockholm, reveal that twenty years ago infant mortality in the upper and middle classes in Stockholm had already declined to not quite one-third of the level which is still the average for the country as a whole. It appears thus to be fully reasonable that with an intensified social policy in the direction of child welfare we could reduce the general national average to the same level, which would mean that about three thousand children could be saved annually throughout Sweden. Measures for the improvement of child welfare are thus by no means lacking in importance even from the quantitative point of view. The well-known general rule that a relation exists between the figures of births and of infant mortality must, however, be borne in mind: with an improvement in the infant mortality rate, a number of births — of children to replace others who had previously died — would, it can be stated with some certainty, not take place.

Approximately ninety thousand children are born in Sweden every year, and as this represents a net reproduction of less than 75 per cent, it is nevertheless apparent that only a relatively small portion of the net reproduction deficiency can be compensated in this way. Assume that with the best child welfare and the lowest child mortality an increase of the net reproduction figures by approximately 3 to 4 per cent is possible. This would imply that these efforts to take better care of infants were certainly not without importance in the quantitative population problem, but that they could meet this problem only to a slight extent.

It is furthermore apparent that a higher marriage rate — assuming that the additional marriages were of the same fertility as the others — would be able to improve the reproduction rate considerably. Likewise, a lower marriage age would tend to raise fertility in marriages.

In my population policy laboratory, Sweden, the marriage rate is unusually low and the average marriage age is high (in first marriages an average age of 29.47 years for men and of 26.50 years for women, in the period 1931–35). The likelihood of contracting marriage is less in Sweden than in most countries. At the ages of thirty, forty, and fifty years, for example, 41, 25, and 22 per cent respectively of all women are unmarried, and at the age of seventy-five to eighty years more than 17 per cent are still unmarried. In Denmark only 15 per cent of women at the age of fifty are unmarried — the Swedish figure was 22 per cent — and in France, which has an especially high marriage rate according to western standards, only 10 per cent. As a consequence, the share of unmarried persons in the total population of Sweden is very large. In 1935 only 49 per cent of the population over fifteen years of age were actually living in marriage; some additional 8 per cent had formerly been married. In the same year, of all men between twenty and thirty-five years old, nearly 70 per cent were unmarried; and of women in the same ages, nearly 60 per cent were unmarried.

Whether a spontaneous increase in marriages can be counted upon appears, however, to be very uncertain. Birth control is increasing, and the knowledge of reliable technical preventive methods is becoming wider, and indeed these factors, especially the latter, will in themselves broaden the possibility of marriage, particularly in youth. Quite a number of these extra marriages, however, will probably aim at intensive birth control. Even though it must be assumed that these marriages will increase the number of births over the number of illegitimate births for which those persons would otherwise have been responsible, it is possible, nevertheless, that they may reduce the average marital fertility.

On the other hand, the advance of rational methods of birth control also gives rise to a contrary tendency, that fewer marriages will be contracted. Many marriages are still occasioned by reason of the fact that extra-marital sexual relations have brought about a conception which the parties wish to legalize. An impression of the importance of this factor can be obtained from the information that, during the period 1926–30, as many as 26 per cent of all births to married women under the age of thirty years took place within eight months after the marriage. Other than first-born children are included in this figure. Had it been possible to base the calculation on first-born children alone, the proportion would have been much greater. Somewhat more direct information is contained in the proportion of all marriages in all age groups which resulted in births within eight months. This proportion was 33.05 per cent for the year 1925. For 1935 it had dropped to 26.82 per cent.

It thus appears probable to me that, even in a country with such a low marriage rate as Sweden — and still more in other countries — great expectations cannot be entertained of any spontaneous increase in marriages, and still less can any great increase in the birth rate be expected on this basis. On the other hand, it is equally apparent that in modern times, when large average families constitute an object which cannot very successfully be pursued, population policy must aim in the first place at an increased marriage rate. It is naturally with respect to unmarried adult citizens that the greatest field for an increased reproduction opens itself. If the commonly accepted view that marriage is a happy form of life is correct, then population policy can with so much the better conscience be directed along this line.

For the present I shall content myself in this matter by pointing out that what the state can do to increase the marriage rate consists chiefly of the same kind of social reforms to ensure the social and economic basis for marriage and the family as are also of importance for the increase of fertility in marriage.

I thereby arrive at what is still the main point in population: How can the uninterrupted decline in fertility in marriages be prevented, and how can the birth rate be raised to the level that is requisite to achieve a balance between births and deaths?

It should here be pointed out at the outset that a fairly large proportion of births takes place under such conditions that in a democratic country, despite the precarious population situation, their preclusion is not only of individual but of social interest. To these *undesirable* births belong, to begin with, the very largest proportion of extra-marital births, which, in my reference country, Sweden, still amount to considerably more than 10 per cent. Children should grow up in normal families. All social experts are agreed that illegitimate births should be prevented to the greatest possible extent. The advance of rational and effective methods of birth control also implies that, quite spontaneously, these births are now being strongly reduced. With the spread of sexual education, for which we are striving, there follows a rapid disappearance of the problem of the illegitimate child.

To the category of undesirable births also belong a very large number of births in wedlock — all those cases in which illness and weakness on the part of the mother, poverty, bad hereditary characteristics, or unsuitable environmental factors exist. Above all, a circumstance which still exists in every country must be abolished — that very large numbers of children are born to poverty-stricken, ignorant parents.

Even in Sweden, where the standard both of living and of public education is relatively high and net reproduction at a very low level, it is still the case that there are many very large families and that these large families are far more numerous among the very poorest, least enlightened, and least advanced social groups than in classes that are economically better situated and culturally more advanced. Thus it happens — I limit myself to only a few illustrative statistics — that the median income (the family income under which half the number of cases falls) is, in towns, 3,023 Swedish crowns for two-child families but only 2,500 Swedish crowns for seven-child families. In rural areas one-child families have a median income of 1,478 Swedish crowns, while the corresponding figure for nine-child families is 1,088 crowns. The countryside is poorer in general than the urban areas — although not in the same proportion as the figures just quoted suggest, for they imply a general underestimation of incomes, particularly for rural districts — and it also has the majority of families with many children.

Very large families are now rapidly becoming less numerous, and the net reproduction is sinking, largely on account of this development. As I see it, in a democratic country it is impossible to maintain any other opinion than that it is desirable that these large families among the poor and unenlightened should disappear in pace with the improvement in the economic and educational conditions of these classes themselves. It is unreasonable that in a democratic society the survival of the people should be safeguarded by the very poorest being kept poor and ignorant, and giving birth to cruelly large families.

Stockholm marks the directional point of the development in Sweden. In Stockholm a positive correlation between incomes and number of children born to married couples has appeared for many years. However, the negative correlation, which is characteristic of most other places and was true of Stockholm also in earlier times, is apparent there even now among subgroups of the lower strata of the working class. People in Stockholm are thus beginning to have children to the extent that they have the means, but the average net reproduction is hardly more than one-third, although all the extra-marital births, which even in Stockholm are very numerous, and all those in wedlock which occur by accident and under adverse conditions still provide a large field for the advance of birth control.

My first basic principle for population policy in a democratic country — and I am here pointing out one of the major restrictions of a quantitative population policy in a democracy — is, therefore, that a very large number of births must be regarded as *undesirable*, and that solicitude for the balance of reproduction must not lead to diminished efforts on the part of the community to reduce the number of births under adverse conditions. Birth control must, on the contrary, be intensified so to reduce genuinely undesirable births. This principle has been expressly approved by the Swedish Population Commission, as also by the

Danish Commission. If this principle is accepted — which, so to speak, gives Neo-Malthusianism what is due to it — and if it can be learned from statistics of the standard of living how great a proportion of all births, even in a relatively prosperous land with an exceptionally low fertility rate like Sweden, is of this type, there are still greater reasons for the very deepest scepticism concerning the possibility that a population policy under modern conditions can restore the equilibrium between births and deaths.

In a democratic society we cannot accept a way of things whereby the poor, ignorant, and inexperienced maintain the stock of the population. In a democratic society we must definitely direct our attention to the abolition of both poverty and ignorance, that is to say, the very factors which for a long time have stimulated a high birth rate; we must do so even though the abundance of children produced by these factors is the only thing at present which prevents the population situation from being even more catastrophic than it is. In a democratic society we must continue to disseminate and officially sanction, through the schools and adult education, demands for cultural and hygienic standards of living which, for the broad masses of the people with current real incomes, are quite incompatible with a normal family size — that is, with a four-child system — and which therefore directly create motives for increased birth control. On these principles we can accept no compromise. We cannot think of raising the number of children by holding back the advance of civilization. Moreover, it would be impossible even if we wished to do so. A rise and leveling off of the *standards* of living — what people are taught to *want* — always precedes, with us, the rise and equalization of the *level* of living — what people actually *have*.

This is the deepest dilemma in the population policy in democratic countries.

This first principle for a positive population policy in a democratic country, that undesirable births shall be prevented, is closely associated with the second principle, that the birth rate shall not be maintained by the *undesired* births. Birth control must be openly and officially declared to be good in itself, and the self-evident superiority of the most effective means of birth control must then also be recognized to have a positive value.

We ought to make clear to ourselves that there is no choice in this matter in a democratic society. In Sweden we have shown that practically all non-sterile marriages utilize some kind of birth control, that birth control in the overwhelming majority of marriages is carried on through technically unsatisfactory methods, but that a more effective technique is rapidly spreading. Even though we should desire to prevent this expansion of effective techniques of birth control, we should certainly not succeed if we tried.

But we cannot desire it and remain true to the tenets of democracy. In the principal report on the sexual problem, the Swedish Population Commission has shown and openly declared that birth control is not merely necessary in special cases on account of hereditary, medical, hygienic, economic, or other reasons, but that it is normally to be recommended in all non-sterile marriages in order to space out the births and to limit the number of children. In marriages which desire a normal number of children birth control is eminently requisite to space the births so that the mother shall not be overstrained. The Commission, therefore, strongly urged the immediate repeal of the laws hindering the sale of and propaganda for contraceptives, which were inaugurated in 1910 as a vain effort to stop the spread of birth control, which was then commencing to gain speed; and Parliament followed the recommendation. Furthermore, the Commission has presented a comprehensive plan for intensified sexual education through the schools and adult education. Information on rational methods for birth control has been given great space in this proposed sexual education. The idea is that even at school age education in the function of birth control shall be included as a part of all the other information of the real world — though not, of course, education in the technique proper of birth control — and that in the future every growing young man and woman in adolescence shall later be reached by a rational instruction in the technique of rational birth control.

The Commission sees in these reforms an act of human honor and truth. To maintain laws contradictory to people's normal behavior and personal beliefs and to keep young people, or people in backward districts and social groups, from information which is accessible to others is an undermining of the morals of the nation and a violation of the basic principles of a democratic society. We have no other choice than to accept rationalism, and even anticipate it, and build our population policy on that ground.

The Commission sees clearly that the immediate effect of this policy is to decrease the number of undesired births. It recognizes, however, that, as is proved by experience, the spread of rational birth control cannot in the long run be hindered. Further, it gives the reasons why it should not be hindered. A democratic population policy should not take advantage of poverty, backwardness, and lack of information. It must be founded on the principle of voluntary parenthood. The Commission points out that the efforts made hitherto to hinder the spread of rational birth control have had a class bias and that they are partly responsible for the deep-rooted mistrust, particularly in the lower income strata, of the very idea of a population policy. The

Commission ends its principal discussion on this point emphatically: "Only when the whole of this field has been swept clean, when the rightfulness of birth control has been openly recognized and honestly accepted in the different political, ideological, and religious quarters, when in connection with these the reliableness of the applied technique in itself has been recognized for its self-evident value, when all efforts to obstruct sound education in this subject have been liquidated and the trade in contraceptives has been brought entirely into the light — only then will a true groundwork have been created among the young people in all social classes for a new, sincerely endorsed, positive attitude to the population problem, which is the vital question both for individual families and for the nation."

It might be mentioned that this programmatic report of the Commission on the sexual question itself clearly broke the law which then existed forbidding the public recommendation of the use of contraceptives; among other things, it includes as a supplement a handbook on preventive technique. The report was not only unanimously supported by the members of the Commission itself, which, besides a number of experts from the universities, included representatives of all four leading political parties, but was also agreed to by its Advisory Council on Medical Questions and its Council on the Ethics of the Population Problem, in which latter the Church and conservative opinion were strongly represented. The Danish Population Commission has expressed the same views.

I believe this attitude toward birth control to be a necessary component, or rather the very basis, of a positive population policy in a democratic country. But it makes all the more difficult the problem of how it shall be possible not only to maintain the present average fertility but also to raise it so considerably as to achieve a new equilibrium between births and deaths.

In this way democracy is forced to make its task in population policy most difficult. There is no way around the principles just expounded. The task is so to alter the basis of the institution of the family in our society that the ordinary citizen, educated to high standards of culture and hygiene and well-informed in the technique of rational birth control, voluntarily chooses to aim at a family with four children.

The discussion of the means of such a positive population policy ought naturally to be based on an analysis of the causes of the spread of extreme birth control. In the present summary, however, I must abstain from such an analysis. I shall only point out in passing that the progress of birth control in Sweden, as everywhere else in the western world, obviously stands in very close relation to the industrialization and rationalization of economic life as a whole and its repercussions on the institution of the family. The deepest dilemma of democratic population policy is that we do not desire, and even if we desired could not hope to accomplish, a reversal of industrialization and rationalization.

My point of departure is hereafter the following. The economic motive for birth control is very clear and very decisive. A child, or another child, means an increased economic burden and, consequently, a lower standard of living. In the modern industrial society, in contrast with the old peasant society, children for the most part imply increased expense but not a rising family income. The cost of children has a tendency to rise with the urbanization of life and increased cultural demands. It may seem peculiar, from this point of view, that there is ordinarily such a close negative correlation between number of children and economic status. Two things must be borne in mind, however: first, the fact that it is a question of differential cost — a child or another child presses down the level of living which otherwise would be possible in all income strata; and second, and most important, that rational birth control is still spreading in society. The practice is sinking down through the social structure, i.e., starting in the higher strata and slowly making its way down to the lower strata. The final outcome — a positive correlation between fertility and economic status — is already visible in some Swedish cities, particularly Stockholm. But then the aggregate fertility is far below full reproduction.

I do not believe that the economic motive is the only one, but I think it is basic. In this respect there is a very striking conflict between the individual and the collective interest. For the population as a whole, the age groups to be supported include the aged as well as children; in the individual family, on the other hand, normally only the children need support. The relative cost of supporting them is constantly rising with urbanization and the increased demand for hygiene and culture.

Old people nowadays are supposed to live on the savings they have made. The conflict between individual and social interests is accentuated by the fact that more and more the old-time three-generation family is being replaced by the two-generation family, and by the fact that to an increasing extent society is taking over the support of the aged when their own means are too small to afford a decent livelihood. The idea that children should support their old parents later in life has more and more lost its grip over ordinary people. The expectation of having to rely on support from grown-up children is, in any case, not a natural and pleasant one. While, therefore, practically all married people try to limit the number of their children to some extent in order to defend the family standard of living, and while an increasing number of them carry out this limitation to the extreme, practically no one breeds children as an investment in order to secure support in old age. Parents do not look upon children as a pension policy.

Here is focused the conflict of interests and motives between the individual family and the social group of families constituting a nation. An increased shifting-over to society of the burden of supporting the aged has a strong psychological and political basis, and will in all probability be continued. The aged have votes; children and the unborn do not. All people imagine themselves as growing old and, eventually, in need of support; they therefore easily identify themselves with the interests of the old; but all people do not expect to be parents, at least not to many children. In the common opinion nobody is himself responsible for his coming into this world; if he has lived and worked he has a "right" to support when he is getting old, even if he has no means of his own. This is the psychology of the taking-over by society of the responsibility for the security of the aged. The individual, on the other hand, is supposed to have primary responsibility for the children to whom he has "voluntarily" given life. This is the principle of individual responsibility for one's own children, an attitude which has lately had its psychological basis tremendously stratified through the very fact of the availability of rational birth control.

In this distinction between the economic effects of bearing children, as these effects appear when looked at from the point of view of the national household and from the point of view of the individual family, lies the burning question of population, so far as this question is an economic one. The distance between these viewpoints — and the conflict between the direct and indirect economic effects of extreme birth control on the economy of families — is constantly being increased by almost all changes going on in modern society. In principle there are two ways by which this distance can again be diminished and the conflict resolved: either (1) the burden of supporting the aged must be laid effectively upon the individual young families (by abolishing the whole structure of social policy enacted to support old and needy persons — and, do not forget, by actually denying them the right to live on their own savings), or (2) a large part of the economic burden of bringing up children must be passed from the individual family to society as a whole, i.e., the burden must be supported by all citizens as taxpayers, the costs of children, in other words, being distributed among the citizens in proportion to their ability to pay taxes, not according to the number of their children. Only the second alternative needs, of course, to be given practical discussion in modern democratic countries.

The general method of population policy can, therefore, be described as a transfer of income from individuals and families without children to families with children. This principle is obvious and is generally agreed upon by all authors on the subject. The present population development will undoubtedly come to change the emphasis entirely in the discussion of economic distribution. Economic analysis thus far has been restricted, on the whole, merely to the distribution between different occupational and social groups. In the future the family point of view will be introduced in the economic theory of distribution as being equally or even more important.

But even if we thus agree on the necessity of a certain redistribution of income within the population in order to mitigate the decrease in level of living which under modern conditions results from having children, only a very small part of the problem is solved. By what means shall this income transfer be accomplished? I have the feeling that the intensive study of this practical problem, which naturally implies a great deal of family sociology and social policy in general, constitutes the most original and the most important contribution of our population investigations in Sweden.

A detailed recapitulation is out of the question here, but mention must be made of some general principles as to the means of the income-transfer desired which have guided our new population policy in Scandinavia. First, while the motive for population policy in the totalitarian countries has been crudely declared to be to "stimulate" the breeding of children, we have argued, in a more sophisticated and roundabout way, that we only wanted to take away the obstacles preventing ordinary persons from following their natural urge to marry and to have children. I can understand if the reader does not quite see the difference. The difference is, however, not a mere play on words. To it corresponds a very important difference in the whole approach to the practical policy. We want a much more profound change in the social and economic basis of the institution of the family. The matter will be clarified in what follows.

Second, we say — and I think that this statement must also be included among the principles of population policy in a democratic country — that we are just as much, and even more, interested in the physical, intellectual, and moral quality of the population as in its quantity. Now, at least in Sweden with its very homogeneous population, quality does not depend on racial differences between population groups but on their environment, especially on the living conditions of the younger generation. From the data we have obtained through our intensive studies of the level of living in families of different sizes in different income groups, it is clear that a very great increase in the quality of future generations would be secured if we only could provide families having children with better housing, nutrition, health care, education, and similar aids to sound development.

One of the significant principles that has now become firmly rooted in Swedish population policy is that quantitative and qualitative aims go hand in hand, without the possibility of coming into real conflict. If, relying on the taxpayer, we take care of the various needs of the family, the result will be not only a higher standard of welfare for the children and a higher standard of quality in the next generation, but also the equalizing of the economic burden of breeding children and consequently of the levels of living in families with and without children. As so very much is still lacking in child welfare in every country, we can safely direct all our population policy upon the qualitative aim and use the quantitative aim only as a broad and general extra argument for all such reforms.

Child welfare also has a quantitative effect in two other ways: by reducing infant mortality and assuring the welfare of children. In the latter respect it has been made clear that a large number of would-be parents, apart from the purely economic motive for extreme birth control, avoid bringing children into the world from a sense of responsibility to these possible children, who, they fear, would run the risk of meeting too severe and degrading conditions of development.

In practice, therefore, the population policy will turn out to be simply an intensification of the important part of social policy which bears upon the family and children. Such a policy is prophylactic rather than palliative or symptomatic: it seeks prevention, not mere cure.

At this point I must halt for a moment and make some observations upon the general line of development of social policy. In its first stage of development social policy is confined to the search for remedies. The immediate demand is for measures to be instituted for the care of the directly necessitous — the poor, the sick, the aged, the unemployed, invalids, alcoholics, psychopaths, prostitutes, criminals, and the members of all such socio-pathological groups. This is mere justice and charity. Only when this curative social policy gets more or less under way can scope be given in a greater degree to prophylactic preventive efforts.

In my reference country, Sweden, social policy has come through its initial phase. In fact, the kind of social policy which I have called curative, though it has not been carried as far as is needed, is at least fairly well-developed. It is thus quite logical to consider ourselves to be on the threshold of a new epoch in social policy in which we shall continue more boldly to strive not only to alleviate distress and cure defects but also, what is vastly more important, to prevent them.

Such a prophylactic policy must naturally and necessarily be directed at the family and at the children who are the people of the future. Such a policy is in a high degree an "investment," an investment in the personal capital of the country. It can be defended, therefore, not only on grounds of charity and justice, like the older type of social policy, but also on the grounds of national conservation of human capital. This investment in personal capital can be even more profitable than investment in factories and machines and other property which rust can corrupt and the moth consume. The principal part of the wealth of a nation always lies in the quality of its population. What I have said here means that when we transfer the emphasis from curative to preventive social policy we must cease to regard the costs of social policy as unprofitable, nonproductive consumption costs on the public budgets. This development in social policy arises quite independently of the population crisis, but the population problem comes at a very timely stage and constitutes a strong stimulus for reforms of a sort which have social and economic purposes within themselves.

Such a broadly prophylactic social policy implies that the state will invest money and care even in families who are not economically distressed. Since, furthermore, the quantitative population argument speaks for a general equalization of the economic burden of bringing up children, there is all the more reason to abandon and reject as far as possible all forms of "means tests," and to look upon this policy not primarily as poor relief but more generally as a democratic and coöperative organization of national consumption motivated by reasons of economic rationality and of efficiency, and of collective solidarity and responsibility within the whole nation for the rising generation. Such a change, from poor relief to general coöperation, has, of course, very great financial implications and cannot be accomplished at once. The tendency, however, is clearly visible in the present activity in the sphere of social reform in Sweden; and the population argument has been the most potent force behind the speeding up of this important transition in social policy from curative to prophylactic, from consumptive to productive, from the aid of the needy to broad coöperation among all the people.

This linking together of the qualitative and the quantitative aims in population policy and, further, of population policy as a whole with the still broader prophylactic social policy motivated by general reasons of social welfare and national economy has also been of great political importance in the fight to create a positive interest in the heart of the people for the fate of the population. Many citizens whom it would certainly be difficult to induce to adopt a positive attitude in the population question — on account of old prejudices, lack of intellectual capacity, or other reasons — reveal an immediate understanding when they see that the means of achieving this policy correspond to what they have already been striving for on other grounds for decades.

This association of objectives also solves the otherwise difficult problem of how to combine the horizontal redistribution of income between different types of families and the vertical redistribution between different income classes. The solution is: certain services free for all children and for all families in all economic classes, with no means test, planned as a rational coöperation between citizens in a democratic society on the principle of national solidarity, financed through the national budget, and, therefore, paid for according to the prevailing principles for the distribution of taxation according to capacity and ability.

What is thus developing is nothing less than a socialization or nationalization of certain important parts of consumption, a carrying over from the individual family budget to the public budget of cost items relating to children. The intended redistribution is carried out in *kind* instead of in *cash.*[1] Such measures can be integrated in a much more rational way than cash allowances into the wider economic policy — agricultural policy, housing policy, and above all business cycle policy and unemployment policy. To a large extent the needs of families and children can be met by engaging otherwise unemployed or underemployed factors of production in work and the whole program engineered in the direction of stabilizing the economic system. This implies that only a portion of the costs should rightly be counted against the social policy involved. As this social policy in itself has the nature of national investment, the measures are the more truly profitable in the collective or national economic calculus.

Given these premises, (1) that a redistribution of total income resources in a population to the advantage of children shall be effected, (2) that quality of population shall be consid-

[1] A comprehensive list and a short discussion of the reforms actually carried out in Sweden as a result of the crises of opinion in population is given by A. Myrdal in *International Labour Review*, June 1939, "A Swedish Programme for Family Security." For an intensive analysis of the problems involved, see A. Myrdal's forthcoming book.

ered the aim in addition to and above quantity, (3) that population policy shall be incorporated in the transformation of social policy from curative and symptomatic to preventive and prophylactic, and (4) that the measures shall be rationally integrated in a planned national economic policy, a most important complex of technical problems of constructive social engineering is raised.

Not even a survey of these socio-technical problems will be attempted in the present volume. One point, however, should be stressed: these problems are problems of social science proper. They can, and they should be treated by means of strictly scientific analysis; the relevant facts must be assembled and penetrated, the aims must be defined, and, on the basis of these premises, plans which are the scientific conclusion from ascertained facts and postulated valuations must be formed. The country is unfortunate, and the democracy poor, where these technical political problems are not dealt with as regular and important parts of the scholarly work of scientists. The scientific discussion ought to be in advance of politics. It ought to grasp problems even before they reach actuality and formulate them in a way intelligible to the general public. Only thus can the scholar lead public opinion and by his initiative give a realistic setting and a rational shape to political questions as they arise. From this point of view it is a particularly discouraging experience to meet the superior attitude of so many social scientists who disclaim any interest in social reform and who usually at the same time depreciate "reformers." It is, indeed, a most remarkable situation in which the constructive technical planning for social change is considered unworthy of the scientist's exertions and left to politicians, reformers, people with panaceas, and other ignominious persons regularly referred to slightingly in scientific literature, while it is obviously considered to be highly suitable for academic science to record minutely the legislative outcrop of these inferior impulses.

Politics is the task of determining what changes are to be induced in the whole system of social institutions. When in a democracy the ultimate power to make this determination is left to all citizens, the idea is that the direction of change should be decided in accordance with prevalent valuations and interests. In order that the changes shall not falsify the true valuations and interests of the common citizen, he needs knowledge; in complicated modern society all changes need careful, detailed planning. This task of planning is a truly scientific one.

The situation may be that public opinion is so uneducated and indifferent, and the politicians so inept, that rational scientific construction is ignored. It may be that the scientists are not accepted as technical engineers or not trained properly to function in such capacities. Such a situation is laden with danger for democracy, which must assume enlightened and rational politics. But in any case it does not excuse scientists for shunning practical problems. If they find their work difficult in the face of a society which does not accept their aid or find themselves untrained for the task, it is a poor escape to rationalize this situation into contempt for the important part of statesmanship which rightly belongs to practical social science.

VIII

POPULATION POLICY AND THE MORAL ISSUE

IN THE discussion of these distributional reforms, carried out through the legislative power of the state, by which the differential cost of having children is spread out among the citizens in conformity with their capacity to pay, one general question is always raised which can never fully be answered: To what degree will such measures actually affect marriage rate and fertility?

It must be remembered that this question is not a crucial one for the type of family reforms here envisaged as constituting the economic ingredients in democratic population policy. The reforms are primarily motivated as investments in the happiness, health, and productive quality of the rising generation and should from this point of view be undertaken even if their quantitative effects upon the population trend were slight.

As a substitute for a direct answer on the question, it should further be pointed out that the effects will depend upon the actual scope of the reforms. A family policy which succeeded in completely eliminating the differential cost of having children should certainly have a rather high degree of effect, quantitatively, on the population. When discussing the reforms which actually are carried out we ought, however, to guard ourselves against illusions.

The family reforms which are now in effect in Sweden, after a rather decided crisis of opinion in the population problem which for a short time caused a sort of national front on this question, are certainly radical compared with the measures advocated by responsible social reformers a few years ago. But even in that country these reforms — some of them already carried out, others in process — are relatively insignificant in their effect upon the difference in levels of living in families with different numbers of children. It must also be borne in mind that a curative social policy was well under way in Sweden, so that, even apart from the population situation, the ground was well prepared for preventive family reforms.

They go in the right direction, it is true, but they are quite modest in scope viewed as population policy.

General opinion is certainly not ready for more far-reaching reforms. As I emphasized in an earlier chapter, there is, on the contrary, reason to expect that for some time there will be a certain diminution in interest in the population problem. The problem, however, will again come to the fore, and then in a more definitive way. In this later period distribution reforms of quite another magnitude will probably become possible. But even these reforms, which in fact would comprise a radical alteration in the whole social structure, probably cannot completely eliminate the differential costs of having children.

Moreover, it is widely recognized — and in fact not denied by anyone — that the limitation of children has other causes than the economic motive. Under all conditions four children means for a wife a heavy personal burden and a hindrance to working and earning money, to social and political aspirations, to sport and dancing, and similarly to everything else she might wish to undertake outside of a sedentary family existence. The general setting of family life developed in modern society, which for a long time has been inimical to having children, is such that a four-child family gets into all sorts of difficulties. Part of this setting can be changed by social reform, and a considerable number of the measures now being taken in Swedish population policy have a wider aim than decreasing the cost of the individual child and raising the environmental standard of children. Stated in a crude way, they also attempt to decrease the hindrance, particularly to mothers, to pursuing other interests within and outside the family. The goal has been set to defend the right of women to work in the labor market and to hold full citizenship in our more and more diversified national culture and, at the same time, to have children. Under these circumstances not only budget items but also important family functions have to be cut from the quasi-paternalistic family of this transitional period and be transferred to the wider national household. In this respect the principle of preferring a national redistribution *in natura* instead of allowances in cash is of foremost importance.

The rebuilding of the economic basis of the institution of the family implies much more than is apparent merely from the distributional aspect.

But even so, and even though these reforms in the future are carried out boldly in the face of all sorts of lagging conventions with deep emotional roots in wishful traditionalism, if the four-child family is again to become normal it is necessary that private attitudes toward marriage and rearing of families be changed. With this I come to what is usually termed the "moral" element in the population problem.

In popular discussions the moral element has customarily been used as an argument against distributional reforms. In many quarters, and not only the very conservative ones, the statement that the population problem is a "moral," or "spiritual," or "psychological" problem and not an economic one again and again has served as an excuse for attempts to evade costly reforms. This whole line of thought is peculiar and doubtful for several reasons.

First, it seems clear that the changes in

private family attitudes which have occurred during the last two generations, and which have generally implied a greater degree of rational deliberation in matters of childbearing, have been synchronous with and a function of the industrial development. This development has constantly increased the relative cost of having children for the individual family and decreased the burden of supporting the aged, and thus, as we have shown, has widened the conflict between collective and individual interests in childbearing. It seems probable at the outset that no social change could modify these attitudes in a direction favorable to childbearing more successfully than distributional reforms restoring the lower differential cost of having children that prevailed in preindustrial society. It is, therefore, difficult to see the logic of juxtaposing the need of mental changes and proposals for economic reforms. I am, then, assuming that on the whole it is not possible, or in any case not desirable, to make people less rationally deliberate — an assumption which I conceive of as a basic valuation implied in western democratic culture.

Second, it should be noted that in a democracy, where sovereignty resides in the entire people, more positive family ideals, at least on the collective or political plane, are a necessary condition for the carrying out of the economic reforms. The majority of every population, and the great majority in a population where birth control has gone as far as it has in the western democracies, consists of citizens who are either unmarried or have no or only very light child burdens. If, therefore, these reforms are to be accomplished to a sufficient extent in a democratic land, they will have to be premised upon a force operating upon an ideal of the family such that the majority of people can overcome their narrow personal interests. Otherwise the family social reforms motivated by population policy are very likely to be unpopular with all classes of society and with all political groups. Even from this point of view the juxtaposition of individual "morality" and social reforms seems illogical.

Third, the economic reforms have another and very important relation to individual "morality." The very execution of these reforms is the most powerful means of social propaganda which society possesses to influence popular attitudes. If I may quote the Swedish Population Commission once again, I should like to choose the following summary: "It is thus certain that the reforms in child welfare and family protection will be at the same time a sanction on the part of society upon normally large families and thus will exert a powerful influence for a change in the social value placed upon families and raising children. The family ideal will thereby be given new power in society and with this also new force in shaping the private attitudes and behavior of individuals."

In dealing with the question of how to form a more positive view among people in contemporary democracies toward marriage and the rearing of children, this strong, double connection with reform policies must not be forgotten, the premise as well as the effect of which is a change in the popular attitude toward the family.

However, there is naturally every reason to seek even more directly to influence private individuals in favor of marriage and the rearing of children. In a democracy there are, it must be remembered, a whole series of limitations which must be observed in conducting such population propaganda.

For one thing, as has already been said, undesirable and undesired births should be prevented, rather than increased, by the dissemination of such information. The propaganda must emphasize the aspect of responsibility in voluntary parenthood. It must not seek to influence poor people to have children whom they cannot offer a healthy home environment.

Secondly, and more importantly, there can never be talk of appealing to the citizen's feeling of "duty" to the nation to have a family and raise children. Complete respect in a democracy must be shown to the individual's freedom and personal integrity. Propaganda which appeals to civic "duty" would, moreover, in all probability be quite ineffective. Having children is an especially private matter. In the long run there is no country in which individuals will marry and have children out of a sense of duty. A people which would reproduce itself out of a sense of duty is a people of robots, a mentally impoverished race.

In the population discussion during recent years in Sweden, to bring the argument back to the country I have used as a point of reference, we have never thought or talked in terms of "duty to the nation." Families ought to have children not in obedience to the good of the State but for their own private happiness. This approach not only corresponds to our democratic ideals but was also deemed to be more effective. Nobody produces children for the State's sake, anyhow.

What a democratic society can do — apart from legislating family reforms to make children less of a burden and a hindrance to private families — is therefore restricted to providing *truthful information and education* to aid private individuals better to understand their own interests. Thus, if it is true that children in a family contribute to the success of marriage, then it ought to be possible to demonstrate this great truth scientifically, or in any case to make it easily and effectively credible.

Empirical researches in this difficult sphere have hitherto been successfully carried out only in a minor degree; they are, however, of the greatest importance. The research observations which have been made seem nevertheless to give some support to the widespread common-sense judgment that in marriages kept childless or nearly so the psychical relations between man and wife tend to be less stable, enduring, intense, and complete. More firmly founded is the proposition that the development situation for the only child is less advantageous than that for the child who grows up with brothers and sisters of about the same age.

The Swedish Population Commission had worked out for its information a careful summary of the findings in the psychological and sociological literature of various countries on these problems. It pointed out the weakness of the material and urged that more work be done in the field. Meanwhile it arrived at the conclusion that the modern miniature family seems to be a rather loose and defective form of institutional organization of personal life for ordinary persons. If economic and other motives for extreme birth control were kept apart, it seemed to the Commission that the size of family prescribed as the goal in the population policy would also be preferable from the point of view of what best guarantees happiness for ordinary parents and children. The Commission pointed out that as the effects in this respect are not so directly obvious to individuals when they are young, particularly as a judgment involves a consideration of remote as well as immediate effects, it was of great importance that these questions should be given their due place in education.

It should be noticed that deliberations like these move on a rational plane and start out from individual happiness. Propaganda in a democracy must not mislead people: it must be truthful; and free criticism will work so that only the truth will prevail. Through the powerful agency of school and adult education, rational views on family life can be spread throughout the growing generation of the nation. The necessity for freedom of discussion, and for basing public propaganda on true information, makes it seem *in the short view*, truly enough, that our hands are bound, while the dictatorships may freely permit the end to justify the means, and at their pleasure prune, add to, or otherwise alter the truth. But it is the ideal ground upon which our whole governmental system rests that *in the long view* the truth, guaranteed by free criticism, is nevertheless more effective.

INDEX

INDEX